ALLEN COUNTY PUBLIC LIBRARY

FORT WAYNE, INDIANA 46802

You may return this book to any agency, branch,
or bookmobile of the Allen County Public Library.

Robert R. Carkhuff, Ph.D.

HUMAN PROCESSING AND HUMAN PRODUCTIVITY

**HUMAN RESOURCE
DEVELOPMENT PRESS**

Allen County Public Library
Ft. Wayne, Indiana

*Copyright © 1986 by
Human Resource Development Press, Inc.*

*22 Amherst Road
Amherst, Massachusetts 01002
(413) 253-3488
1-800-822-2801*

First Edition, First printing, April 1986

**Library of Congress Cataloging in Publication Data
International Standard Book Number 0-87425-037-4**

Cover Design by Dorothy Fall
Composition by The Magazine Group
Printing and Binding by Bookcrafters

TO B.R. BUGELSKI
who introduced me to learning theory
and the logic of scientific inquiry

2311743

About The Author

Dr. Robert R. Carkhuff is numbered among the 100 most-cited social scientists according to the Institute for Scientific Information. He also has contributed three of the 100 most-referenced social science texts, including his two-volume masterpiece on *Helping and Human Relations*.

In the private sector, Carkhuff heads Human Technology, Inc., one of the fastest growing corporations in the country, having averaged more than 100% growth per year over the past seven years. In so doing, he has directed more than 500 projects impacting human performance and human productivity. Carkhuff has recorded his understanding of individual performance and organizational productivity in two of his most recent works, *Sources of Human Productivity* and *The Exemplar*.

In the public sector, Carkhuff chairs the Carkhuff Institute of Human Technology, a nonprofit institute which, under the direction of Dr. David N. Aspy, has been responsible for conducting hundreds of research and demonstration programs involving hundreds of thousands of people in developing human resources. In education, most recently, he has authored *The Productive Teacher*, and *Productive Thinking Skills*. In the social sciences, he has written the classics, *The Development of Human Resources*, and *Toward Actualizing Human Potential*.

Preface &
Acknowledgements

I have intended this work for innovators and field leaders concerned with human resource development in both the private and public sectors; students as well as teachers; trainees as well as trainers; delivery personnel as well as managers and supervisors. In this regard, I believe that education and business have the heaviest burden of responsibility in learning to process productively. Together, they converge upon the economic productivity and individual freedom that promise both individualism and humanism in a peaceful world.

In completing this series, I am indebted to the following people:

- Dr. Bernard B. Berenson who consulted on the original design.
- Dr. John R. Cannon, Mr. Alex Douds, Ms. Sharon Fisher, Dr. Richard Pierce and Dr. Ray Vitalo who helped critique the model.
- Drs. Berenson and Selma Wasserman who critiqued the manuscript.
- Dr. John R. Cannon and Ms. Sharon Fisher who edited the manuscript.
- Drs. David N. and Cheryl B. Aspy and Dr. Flora Roebuck who transformed human processing skills into teaching and learning applications.

In developing these principles of learning, I have, myself, been learner as well as teacher. I am the grateful recipient of the teachings of the following people—my colleagues, friends and teachers:

- Dr. David N. Aspy who taught the primacy of people.
- Dr. James W. Becker who taught the necessity of systems thinking.
- Dr. Bernard G. Berenson who taught the power of higher-order processing.
- Dr. David H. Berenson who taught the value of instructional technology.
- Dr. Terry Bergeson who taught the commitment of the educator.
- Dr. B. Richard Bugelski who taught the potency of learning theory.
- Dr. James Drasgow who taught inclusiveness before exclusiveness.
- Dr. Andrew H. Griffin who taught caring as the source of "making a difference."
- Dr. Shirley McCune who taught equity and access as critical ingredients of opportunity.
- Dr. Margaret Jones who taught the critical nature of early childhood education.

I owe a particular debt of gratitude to the following people:

- My parents, Hilda and Bob Carkhuff, who taught me my fundamental values, most basic of which were freedom and the primacy of intellect, and which have guided me throughout my life.
- My wife, Bernice, who has been a source of nourishment and support throughout my adult life, and without whose facilitative effort in management, development and production this work would never have been completed.

McLean, Virginia   Robert R. Carkhuff, Ph.D.
March 1986

Foreword

The conditioned response numbs awareness and renders volition a memory. Even in the midst of wonderous technology, the magic of a never-ending flow of information, relationships that nourish, conflicts that provide new challenge, and dreams of what can be, we continue to rest and seek the comfort of our conditioned responses.

Now, more than ever in our brief history, we must address the grand nature of the individual. Every so often in our history, we have stood at a threshold of understanding more about our world and the universe. Crossing those thresholds has taken us from our small villages to exploring space, the nature of energy, and life itself. We have rarely stood at a more important threshold than understanding more about what we are, what we can be, and of what we can do. A fundamental understanding of our humanity has eluded us, perhaps because of our search for the impossible condition of stability. For the first time we can choose to work with and create with change.

Dr. Robert Carkhuff teaches us we are one with and separate from nature simultaneously. Our humanity makes that seemingly impossible state possible. Our humanity, rooted in our intellect, composes an evolving reality forged out of apparently opposed materials and events: subjective and objective, inclusive and exclusive.

This paradox and its evolving configuration becomes most interesting when Carkhuff asks us to consider that our development may depend upon reaching beyond both the subjective and objective in order to develop perspective and skills that yield a higher, more unifying consciousness.

"Human Processing" helps us to learn how to include the foreign and, where appropriate, exclude the familiar and comfortable. The reader will realize a new psychology that can be the property of every person, yet is basic enough to nourish the unique characteristics of us. What is left unsaid is that without such an actualization of our humanity, supported by the full potential of our intellect, humans may not realize a future.

There is however more than technology in these pages; there is morality and ethics. In the past we have universally made heroes out of those who cut corners and even those who cheat publically. In a sense, throughout history one could not be too dishonest as long as that dishonesty paid off in profit and property. Carkhuff shares the tools that will make it impossible to be *too* honest in the ages of information.

The crisis is in choosing whether or not to be human. In the past we have chosen to be less. Psychodynamic reasons and excuses for being less no longer apply. Psychotherapy may be a curiosity of history.

The cumulative and developmental operations in this work may lead to a capacity to trust our own eyes, define our own goals and act upon what we see and what we value, rather than what we are conditioned to see and want. When we can see with our own eyes, and want what we value, we will be free and fully human enough to actualize an expanding, vital human family full of achieving, loving brothers and sisters. Then we will choose the best for the human family and we will come to know that there can be no poison in human intimacy.

Productive thinking may rid us, once and for all, of our neuroses. There will be no dichotomies to explain away our ignorance and vanities. Productive thinking skills help us to change our definition of ego from sensitized to sensitive; from independent to interdependent. There will no longer be in our explanations of nature and experience, constants to numb us into an imagined sense of stability. Most important of all, the best and the worst we can do will be the same: productive.

Carkhuff facilitates the actualization of the individual's freedom to exercise judgment with perspective, empathy and love.

Now we can learn the skills to re-examine our issues, to care enough to examine our intra- and interpersonal histories, develop a willingness to be free and understand the power in diversity. We can learn how diversity may enable us all to create the time to reach fullness as humans.

Carkhuff lends us new ways to represent our experience, to blend the diversity of the physical universe with that of our individual dynamics. He initiates a process for representing the interdependent nature of our human family as the connective tissue of our potential to discover, build, and care. And—these pages give us new ways to teach our children that time is both physical and dynamic. They can create their own time!

With the skills to think productively, moment to moment, application and transfer merge. The products of transfer skills are those only humans can produce: new content, skills, principles, science, models, new integrative philosophy.

This is a major work not only for what it contributes but that it helps us unburden ourselves.

We can all go on to welcome input no matter what the source *and* still be attracted to the source of input.

We now have no choice but to maintain and fine tune our capacity to be surprised.

While human processing can achieve these freedoms, it also nurtures innocence; a freedom from guilt and guile that enables the mind to work naturally with the truth. Carkhuff has discovered the difference between ego-sense and ego-centricity so that we can give up our self-conscious preoccupations.

Every crises is now a crises for us all.

Every contribution is now a contribution to us all. We need to prepare our world to receive processing people, young and old, male and female, of all colors.

We have all the basic material so that we may never again entertain "bailing out." Nourishment and feedback will be constant rather than sporadic. In this context, self management will be a reality, so when individuals interact, the output will increase factorially based upon the number of input units contributed by each of the interacting individuals. Our interactive contributions are truly infinite!

Most important, responding to each other accurately will not only be a reality but a requirement.

There is here in people and their work the modeling of the freedom in discipline and the successful blending of ethics and technology. At the same moment, there has never been a greater emphasis on the central and basic nature of human values. Learning becomes constant because there is a strategy to learn *how* to learn. Acquisition, application and transfer are cumulative and developmental, and application and transfer merge into achievement.

At last we have the tools to minimize perceptual variance while increasing perspective variance. The implications are endless!

The book is a declaration of freedom of choice supported by reason and technology congruent with natural *human* functions.

I have learned from these pages and the author that time is the source of all variance; that variance is the creator of change; and that these relationships represent energy of such magnitude that it dwarfs the power in the atom, reducing it in impact and long-term significance.

Robert Carkhuff leads the way to a new philosophy — and becomes the first philosopher of the new ages of human thinking. He has done this by integrating, even maturing the great traditional issues of philosophy with the pragmatic. He does so out of an expanding yet directed perspective based upon on-going sensory-perceptual input and functionally determined focus: the keys to unlock the gates to never-ending suprise.

Bernard G. Berenson
Hampden, Massachusetts
March, 1986

The Processor

My friend, Jim Becker, warns us that the world is caught in a systems grid-lock. We're in an immense traffic jam with no way in or out, and all the parking spaces are occupied by those who got there first and refuse to move. Our systems—resource, social, political, economic, educational—threaten us with another "Dark Age," one from which we may never recover. Our finite resources have been ripped off, our skies polluted, our streams contaminated, obligating future generations to fund the burden of our excesses, and cheating them of their rightful heritage. Our political systems reflect the greed of their constituents as they commit only to lobbied entitlement policies for big businesses and small minds. The energies of our economic systems are dedicated to protectionism for the past and denial of the future as they revere the meanderings of yet another Neanderthal. Our educational systems produce *consumers* rather than *producers* of information as we rear a generation afraid to fail. All systems feed off of one another in an entropic gorging of primeval appetites.

It is our personal comfort zones which have brought us effectively to the brink of this human precipice. It is our conditioned responses that have sentenced us to intellectually repeat the past. All comfort is ephemeral as it fades with the fulfillment of privatized motives. All conditioning is pathological since it fails to produce the responses required by changing environmental conditions.

There is another way. It is the way of the processor.

It is the way of true scientists who open their content to processing rather than closing it permanently in infinite variations of doomed specialties.

It is the way of the free enterpriser who recognizes the laws of growth as well as the ethic of consumer productivity: "Our business is to keep our consumers in business!"

It is the way of the teacher who relates interdependently to the learners, teaching them everything the teacher knows and, in turn, learning everything the learners know, while searching out sources of expertise which none of them know.

It is the way of the political leader who leads by data-based direction rather than biased public opinion polls, who protects only by freeing and frees only by processing.

The processor is a new ingredient in the annals of humankind. We first met the processor in Plato and Leonardo da Vinci. We recognized the processor in our lifetimes in Einstein and Kilby. Some few now realize that what was demonstrated by them is now required of us—*all* of us!

The processor recognizes that we live on a fragile spacecraft which we call Earth, held together only by our interdependent love. The processor recognizes that human processing is the source of the higher-order processing that will produce infinite human productivity. The processor recognizes that new ideas and deeds are the currency in a global village which knows no boundaries between its citizens who know no walls within their homes.

Only the productive processor—the exemplary performer—can see a way out of our systems grid-lock. The exemplars—if not eliminated or neutralized—show the way by making something out of nothing; by throwing out sky-hooks and pulling themselves up by their own bootstraps; by leaving behind conditioned responders (some of whom may then seek to become more than the few habitual responses they are); and by, above all else, becoming human and in so doing elevating the substance and structure of civilization.

The processor offers another way—a civilized way—indeed the only other way—to break this deadly embrace.

March 1986

R.R.C.
McLean, Virginia

Table of Contents

About the Author
Preface & Acknowledgements
Foreword
The Processor

I. INTRODUCTION AND OVERVIEW   1

    1. Human Conditioning and Human Crises   3
       • The Cultural Contexts   6
         • Industrial and Earlier Eras   7
         • The Electronics Era   8
         • The Information Age   10

II. THE EVOLUTION OF HUMAN PROCESSING   13

    2. Individual Processing Through the Ages   15
       • Processing Approaches   20
         • S→R Conditioning   21
         • S→O→R Learning   24
         • S→P→R Processing   26

    3. Interpersonal Processing Through the Ages   29
       • Directing and Controlling   31
       • Facilitating Processing   32
       • Interdependent Processing   34

    4. Organizational Processing Through the Ages   37
       • Mechanical Processing   39
       • Computer Processing   41
       • Human Processing   43

III. TOWARD MODELS FOR HUMAN PROCESSING   47

  5. Individual Processing in the Age of Information   49
     • Human Processing   52
       • The Skills of Exploring   53
       • The Skills of Understanding   53
       • The Skills of Acting   54
     • The Phases of Human Processing   55
     • The Human Processing Model   56
       • Stimulus Input   58
       • Human Processing   59
       • Response Output   60
       • Feedback   61
     • The Skills of Human Processing   62
     • The Systems of Human Processing   66

  6. Interpersonal Processing in the Age of
     Information   75
     • Individual Processing   77
     • Interpersonal Processing   80
     • "Get, Give, Merge and Go"   81
     • Interpersonal Processing Products   83

  7. Organizational Processing in the Age
     of Information   85
     • Organizational Processing Operations   86
       • Resource Inputs   87
       • Organizational Processing   89
       • Results Outputs   92
       • Information Feedback   93
     • Improving Organizational Productivity   94

IV. R & D IN HUMAN PROCESSING   97

  8. Individual Processing and Individual Performance   99
     • Living and Learning Performance   100
     • Working Performance   107

9. Interpersonal Processing and Unit Productivity   111
 • Productivity Improvement   114
 • Interpersonal Productivity   116
10. Organizational Processing and Organizational
 Productivity   121
 • Surveying Sources of Productivity: Methods   123
  • Corporate Characteristics   123
  • Questionnaires   125
 • Sources of Productivity: Results   128
  • Open-Ended Responses   128
  • Structured Responses   130
  • Comparative Data   132
 • Sources of Productivity: Summary and
  Conclusions   134
  • Organizational Components   134
  • Organizational Functions   135
  • Organizational Processes   135
  • Conclusions   136

V. SUMMARY AND TRANSITION   139

11. Human Processing and Human Productivity   141
 • Sources of Economic Growth   141
 • Sources of Human and Information Resource
  Development   146
 • Toward Human Processing and Human
  Productivity   149
 • Toward Personal Growth   153

APPENDIX   157

Bibliography   159

I.
Introduction and
Overview

1.
Human Conditioning and Human Crises

I have the distinct privilege of being a policy-making executive in an Information Age agency. We are an R & D firm committed to putting technology in the service of humanity. In the process, we are attempting to accomplish not only a human and technological interface; we are committed to creating a "critical mass"—or synergy—within and between the humans and their technologies.

We produce tailored instructional and management systems designs (and the resultant products and services) calculated to improve individual performance and organizational productivity. The project contents may range from state-of-the-art human and information resource development and management systems through multimedia systems (including computer-assisted instruction) to differentiated productivity designs based upon increasingly futuristic scenarios.

Over the past five years, we have implemented about 600 new projects, nearly 200 in the past year, so that we are averaging between three and four new projects per week. Every week there are dozens of iterations of informational input and feedback, the more significant of which are fielded by our chief executive officer. Of these messages, perhaps a dozen may change the direction of any one of our projects from 1° to 180°. At least one message per week may change the direction of our entire agency from 1° to 180°. Indeed,

3

we live on the razor's edge, poised between growth and extinction.

I consider it the most significant of all my learning experiences to have this opportunity to peer into the future. Our problems will be the problems of all other organizations six months or two years from now. Sooner or later, all organizations in the public and private sectors will experience this same press of information. They will either learn to receive information or they will be retarded in their development. They will either learn to process the information they have received or they will deteriorate. They will either dedicate their processed information to increasingly productive outcomes, i.e., simultaneously increasing results outputs while decreasing resource inputs, or they will cease to exist.

The same implications hold for individual personnel. I have found that personnel fall into three categories—conditioned responders, participative learners or fully functioning processors. All experience the enormous press of information input. It is what they do with this press that distinguishes them and their performances.

By far the great majority—the conditioned responders— *limit the information they receive to the wavelengths with which they feel comfortable. For them, it is like setting the dial of their radios or television sets to one particular station. They allow themselves to receive only that input for which they have a response. Or, they make the same response over and over regardless of the informational input. Clearly, these personnel are most effective in dependent roles where they are handed tasks or steps in a program to perform based upon goals determined by others. Because of their inability to "compute" the constantly changing information requirements imposed by the environment, they tend to produce low quality products—late. Ultimately, the conditioned responders are counterproductive, because their limited response repertoires force them to consume increasing levels of resource inputs but produce decreasing levels of results outputs.*

A minority of personnel—perhaps 10% or 20%—fall into the category of participative learners. *They participate in the learning process. They are most effective in considering alternative courses of action to achieve goals, once the data has been analyzed, factored and synthesized. When performing on these terms,* participative learners *can contribute to the definition and achievement of goals. Generally, they produce products of acceptable quality—on time. Although they participate in defining their own goals, ultimately the* participative learners *may become unproductive, due to their lack of comprehensive responsiveness.*

Less than 5% of the personnel—the processors—*elicit and expand their information inputs and sources, process the information by factoring the significant contributions of the information, and then dedicate their processing toward incrementally greater productivity. Not only are they tolerant of the information press, they are committed to expanding its size and variability. They don't just endure the iterations of processing, they enjoy the creative negotiation of their values with any implied requirements of the information. Not only do they subscribe verbally to performance improvement, they increase their productivity exponentially with every iteration of the production cycle, producing infinite results outputs while investing infinitesimal resource inputs.*

The great paradox is that the conditioned responders who avoid or distort the information input to serve their conditioned comfort zones are often very unhappy people. They become aversively conditioned to any information input that does not converge with the responses they already have. They say, "Don't teach me anything I don't already know!" The conditioned responders are the dinosaurs of the Information Age. They are increasingly isolated as they teeter precariously on the edge of extinction.

In turn, the participative learners, nourished as they were by the participative styles of learning and management of the last twenty years, are becoming increasingly anxiety-ridden. They are beginning to recognize the inadequacy of their responses. They do not process the iterations of input and feedback to shape tailored products with maximum effectiveness and efficiency. They are made most anxious by the processors who do process. The participative learners are brought to constant states of crises and tension by the information press. Whether or not they can develop the necessary variability in their learning styles will decide the survival of their species.

Conversely, the processors begin to experience information inputs as a "high." The more input, the more brain activity. The more brain activity, the more "critical mass" of thinking. The more thinking, the more productivity! They are the creators of the Information Age. Their information by-products incessantly move the Age toward its mission: public access to a universal data base that will benefit humankind. Happy and fulfilled, they are increasingly synergistic as they move toward their personal mission: to grow, to become, to fulfill their goals.

These are the three worlds of humankind: one dedicated to preserving the responses it was conditioned to make, making fewer and fewer responses in the face of greater and greater information; another dedicated to participation alone in learning, and spending their entire lives as learners, anxiously recognizing the inadequacy of their responses; and the last group committed to processing the information. Understanding the learning patterns/styles underlying these prototypes is critical. The implications for individual performers, organizations, nations and humanity are profound.

The Cultural Contexts

Learning styles and strategies do not operate in a vacuum. They are responses to the cultural contexts of their times. Actually, they help to frame these cultural contexts. Together the learning styles and cultural contexts define the people and their times.

Several major evolutions in cultural context have occurred in our own lifetimes. First, the so-called Industrial Revolution has been brought to culmination, which bore an even more powerful revolution, the Electronics Era. Now, in turn, the Electronics Era has given birth to a great new Age of Information. The implications of these successive cultural revolutions are profound, not only for the learning strategies of the people who populated these ages, but also for the *humanity* of the people themselves.

It is important to understand these cultural revolutions as developmental and cumulative. For example, we continued farming as the main source of food production even as we entered and exited the Industrial and the Electronics Eras, and now as we enter the Information Era. Similarly, the manufacturing of products continues to underly the evolving service economies of the Electronics and Information Eras. However dramatically our culture changes, we incorporate the contributions of the previous eras in our activities into the current era.

Industrial and Earlier Eras

In humankind's fourteen million year history, the Agrarian Era—which enabled us to move from hunter-gatherers to farmers and herders—is itself only ten thousand years old. Indeed, we can mark the beginning of civilization as we now understand it with the gathering of people in towns and villages in a farming economy. In turn, the Industrial Era is only two hundred years old.

Throughout this history humans were required to make only conditioned responses. The hunter-gatherers' responses were the detailed variations in hunting and gathering. The farmers' responses were the fine elaborations of programs for raising crops and herding animals. The industrial workers' responses were the intricate steps of the manufacturing programs.

In each of these conditioning programs, performers were given information about only those steps which they must

7

complete. To be sure, our social history is derived from the division of labor into linear, technological tasks. This division of labor was most apparent in the modern assembly line where each worker performed a set of tasks based upon previous performance, which implied subsequent performance.

The essence of the cultural contexts during these earlier eras was to give the performer a task to be completed. This was institutionalized by leaders who had their own tasks to perform. Tribal chieftains had to analyze environmental conditions to direct their tribes toward new hunting or gathering grounds. Feudal lords had to analyze growing and rearing conditions to direct their societies toward more fertile farming and husbandry. Captains of industry had to analyze market conditions to direct their industries toward more profitable markets.

In every case, the leaders held the reigns to their operations. They analyzed the relatively stable and unchanging information about relevant conditions. They factored the information into principles which then directed their societies. They handed off information only about the tasks to be performed, and only on a "need to know" basis.

In every case, the people performed as *conditioned responders*. They were conditioned through reinforcement to perform specific responses to specific stimuli. Sometimes, in these resource dependent eras, it took a generation of apprenticeship to learn a few simple responses.

The Electronics Age

The invention of the microprocessor by Jack Kilby in July of 1958 ushered in a new age of organizational productivity and human performance. Derived from the cheapest of all raw materials, sand, the semi-conductor chip made astronomical reductions possible in the size, cost and power requirements of electronic equipment. No longer resource dependent, a single chip driven by inexpensive batteries, was faster, more reliable and more powerful than the largest, most energy-consuming computer of the 1950s. The chip provided enormous productivity leverage and symbolized the productive power of the Electronics Age.

At the same time, the Electronics Age brought with it a set of new requirements, which were imposed upon frequently reluctant personnel. Because of the enormous complexity of electronics circuitry and digital technologies, personnel were required to participate in decision making and goal setting. No longer was it sufficient for people to make their conditioned responses to perform their assigned tasks. Now they had to be involved in determining alternate goals and courses of action to achieve those goals. In effect, personnel were suddenly involved in creating their own assignments.

Typically, personnel were handed the conclusions of data analyses and were asked to help translate these conclusions into day-to-day operations. Participative management became the norm as managers and supervisors considered alternative strategies and then detailed their preferred operations. Quality circles tapped into the conditioned responses of delivery personnel as they shared alternatives and then implemented preferred ways of performing the tasks.

In all of these cases, the Electronics Era personnel functioned as *participative learners*. They shared their expanding repertoires of conditioned responses with each other. Effective processing was defined as matching the appropriate responses to the appropriate discriminative stimuli. These responses were organized in two-dimensional configurations which we termed *systems designs*.

At the same time, the leaders alone retained the rights to analyze the original data bases. The data itself came in waves of increasing intensity and decreasing time. No longer did it take ten years for the information base to change. The data often changed in a matter of months. The leaders controlled their organizations and their destinies by controlling the flow of information. They handed off only their synthesized conclusions as they drove their organizations toward more cost-effective operations.

The Information Age

The Agrarian Era reassured us of the food production necessary to support human survival. The Industrial Age relieved us of exhausting physical labor. The Electronics Era eliminated mind-numbing calculation tasks. Together, these ages provided us with all of the tools we needed to prepare us for the Age of Information.

Now, during that Age, the digital and telecommunication technologies combine to make the world a global village. Communications are instantaneous. The flow of information is continuous. Change is constant. The impact of information is immediate.

Consequently, the demands upon human performance are enormous. We are being asked to continually process the constantly changing data we receive. No longer can we rely upon our repertoire of conditioned responses, however participatively we share them.

Our leaders alone can no longer manage the information flow. More data crosses managers', supervisors', or delivery persons' stations in a day than the Rockefellers or Carnegies were exposed to in a lifetime. In my own area as a productivity consultant, we manage nearly two hundred projects a year. Most of these projects involve months or years of work. Most of these projects involve expenditures of tens or hundreds of thousands of dollars—some, millions. All of these projects demand complex model building in multidimensional space. Freud saw fourteen patients in his lifetime and based his theory of psychoanalysis upon them. Marx predicated his theory of dialectical materialism upon a capitalistic structure that no longer exists. Einstein generated his theories of physics and reality upon limited numbers of observations that for us are expanded exponentially each day.

Perhaps not entirely by choice, personnel at all functional levels are handed entire data bases to process. Most often they receive the data precisely because *they are at the source of information flow*. Indeed, the initiative processors elicit the information they need to process their responses. These personnel require human processing skills.

II.
The Evolution of
Human Processing

2.
Individual Processing Through the Ages

In the early 1970s, IBM field-tested the first version of its computer-based career guidance program, Educational and Career Exploration System (ECES), in Montclair, New Jersey. ECES shared all available career information with secondary students. When ECES was evaluated, no significant differences were found between the treatment and control groups. In other words, those students who received career information were no better off than those who did not in terms of indices such as career decision making and preparation.

When the problem was brought to me by Dr. Ted Friel, one of the developers of the program, I asked a critical question: "Were the students taught how to process the information?" Values processing, decision making, preparation and placement skills were incorporated into the later versions of the ECES system. The newer system was tested in Genesee Intermediate School District, in and around Flint, Michigan, with positive results that encouraged Donald Super, one of the program's original consultants, to label the system "the program of the 1980s." The ECES system continues successfully today in its fifth iteration under the direction of Al Mallory.

The critical learning from this R & D work involved processing. Those students with processing skills benefitted from the information. Those students without processing skills did not benefit from the information.

The ECES experience serves as a paradigm for the Age of Information. By itself, information has little value. At best, it may stimulate processing. At worst, it may be overwhelming. On the other hand, information in the hands of people with processing skills is the most valuable resource input.

Different cultural contexts call for different processing strategies. The different processing strategies then serve to produce or reinforce the different cultural contexts. In other words, the contexts and strategies interact with each other to define the individual and the society.

The Industrial and pre-Industrial Eras required conditioned responses from their performers. The leaders analyzed the data, organized the goals, developed the programs and assigned tasks or steps to be performed. The performers made the specific responses they were conditioned to make to specific stimuli.

In its simplest form, behavior is viewed in terms of a stimulus ⟶ response or S ⟶ R sequence (see Figure 2-1). *There is no intervention between stimulus and response.* When the stimulus is presented, the response is made, similar to the way a knee muscle reflexes to a tap.

Thus, the responses we made at home to our parents or children, those we made in school to our teachers or learners, and those we made at work to our employers or

$$\text{S}\text{timulus} \longrightarrow \text{R}\text{esponse}$$

Figure 2-1. Stimulus and Response in Behavior

employees were all conditioned responses. For our purposes, what is critical is that there is no intelligence or intentionality mediating the sequence or relationship of stimulus and response. The *conditioned responder* simply reacts in an unthinking or mechanical manner. Reduced, the "condition"—or stimulus complex—determines the person's response. Indeed, it is believed by many learning theorists that the cultural or conditioning context determines the behavior of its human populations.

Processing in the Electronics Era was based upon the sharing of conditioned responses. The Electronics Era defined its requirements in terms of "participative learning." The leaders analyzed the data and synthesized the factors directing an organization's activities. The performers "participated" in considering alternative goals and courses of action and in operationally defining these goals and technologically developing the programs to achieve the goals. The performers drew from a repertoire of shared responses to formulate the responses most appropriate to the stimuli.

In this context, the difference between conditioning and learning is the intervening organism:

$$S \longrightarrow O \longrightarrow R$$

The organism intervenes to mediate or transform the stimulus material into appropriate responses. Of course, in order to make an appropriate response, it is assumed that the organism has a repertoire of responses.

Indeed, it is assumed that the individual organism is defined by a set of conditioned responses $(S \longrightarrow R)$ (see Figure 2-2). In other words, the individual acquires a set of responses he or she draws from to respond to the stimuli. Depending upon the stimuli, the individual possesses a hierarchy of responses in readiness to respond. The individual discriminates the stimuli and formulates one or more responses that are appropriate to the stimuli.

Our responses to others at home, school or work are, at once, drawn from our response hierarchy and calculated to facilitate increasing our response hierarchy. It is critical to understand that the intervening organism's "intelligence" is derived from the extensiveness of its repertoire of responses and the accuracy of the ability to discriminate the stimuli. Learning is predicated upon the principle of expanding the response repertoire. Participative learning is predicated upon sharing and participating in selecting responses with others. In some cases, individuals and groups may negotiate new responses based upon an integration of conditioned responses. However, individuals or groups are always limited by their conditioned repertoires of responses.

Finally, processing in the Age of Information incorporated the response repertoires of both conditioned responders

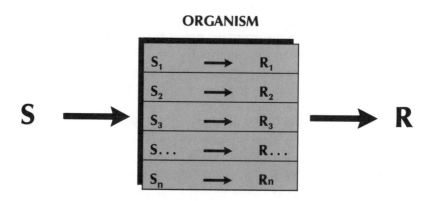

**Figure 2–2. The Response Repertoire
of the Intervening Organism**

and participative learners. The Age of Information both defines and is defined by its requirements: a continuous flow of constantly changing information that demands continuous processing. Leaders and performers are defined individually and interdependently by their ability to transform data into effective responses. Frequently the most effective processor is the delivery person, who is at the greatest point of information flow.

In this context, the organism intervenes to process a response that is quantitatively "greater" or qualitatively "better" than the stimuli were calculated to elicit:

$$S \longrightarrow P \longrightarrow R$$

Put another way, the processor censors his or her conditioned response in order to process incrementally better responses. For that to happen, though, *the processor must have a repertoire of processing responses.*

Basically, it is assumed that the individual processor possesses a hierarchy of conditioned responses based on past experiences. What the individual does with this hierarchy constitutes processing (see Figure 2-3). The individual is

PROCESSING

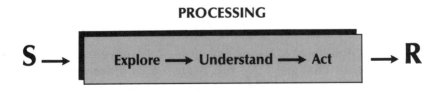

Figure 2-3. The Response of Processing Organisms

able to explore and analyze where he or she is in the stimulus experience. Based upon this exploration and analysis, the individual is then able to understand and define where he or she wants or needs to be: in short, to identify his or her goals. Finally, based upon understanding those goals, he or she is able to act to develop and implement programs to achieve the goals. Processing is recycled with feedback from acting to stimulate more extensive exploring, more accurate understanding and more effective acting.

In living, learning and working contexts, we can transform raw data into productive information. In a very real sense, after the period of analysis and synthesis of the data, the processor has thrown out his or her own personal "sky-hook" in the form of an operational definition of a now-achievable personal objective. In a very real way, processors pick themselves up by their own bootstraps in designing and implementing the individualized programs to achieve their personal objectives.

The difference between *human processing* and *conditioning or learning* is profound. Conditioning allows only the highest-order conditioned response to be made reflexively. Learning intervenes to select a more functional response from an expanded hierarchy of responses. Processing explores the experience, understands the goal, and then acts to achieve it. Human processing is qualitatively different from all forms of conditioning, whether reflexive or participative.

Processing Approaches

The psychology of learning has come to a crossroad. Major theoretical changes have not occurred in more than two decades. The philosophical bases for most current theories have existed since the advent of the Industrial Revolution two centuries ago. But, the world has changed dramatically. The rapid flow of information makes human processing a vital topic of survival and growth. The Age of Information presents the choice squarely before us: facilitate human processing or face extinction in a constantly changing world to which we could not adapt.

Conditioning represents reactive responses to specific environmental stimuli. This stimulus-bound view of humanity relies upon the conditioning history of the responder. It assumes an *unchanging* world, where human development occurs as a monotonic increase in associational complexity.

Learning represents active, expanding responses to variations in the environment. It relies upon the individual's opportunity to share or acquire new responses. It assumes a *slowly changing* world with behavioral options as the products of an internal cognitive structure.

Human processing represents proactive initiatives used to transform the environment. It relies upon an individual's ability to analyze, synthesize and project the probabilities of any future actions, and then to operationalize the goals and technologize the programs for the preferred actions. It assumes a *constantly changing* world where all processors are independently *and* interdependently defined.

As a rule, the unknown is inherently aversive to conditioned responders. They cannot probe what they cannot respond to.

The unknown is existentially acceptable to participative learners. They have been reinforced for transforming it into known, manageable dimensions.

The unknown is attractive to processors. Their mission is to generate the known by projecting the future. They believe that where the brain can project, the body can follow.

S ⟶ R Conditioning

The contributions of the **S ⟶ R** conditioning theories, however limited, are critical. As theorizing advances through learning and processing, the value of conditioned responses are multiplied exponentially. Processors produce new responses from moment to moment when they process any new content. The repertoire of available habitual responses becomes extraordinary.

The contribution of **S ⟶ R** conditioning toward human processing revolves around manipulating the stimulus and response (see Figure 2-4). The rules or operations of stimulus manipulation focus upon the dimension of the stimulus in order to evoke the appropriate response (Bower and Hilgard, 1981; Bugelski, 1956; Hilgard and Bower, 1975; Hilgard and Marquis, 1961; Hull, 1951; Thorndike, 1931). These stimulus operations include the following:

- distinguishing stimulus dimensions quantitatively and qualitatively (Atkinson and Estes, 1963; Carterette, 1961; LaBerge, 1961; Kimble, 1961; Spence, 1956);
- attaching discriminative cues to the dimensions (Lovejoy, 1968; Restle, 1955; Sutherland and Macintosh, 1971; Zeaman and House, 1963);
- prescribing behaviorial guidelines for responding to the dimensions (Ausubel, 1960; Kintsch and VanDijk, 1979; Meyer, 1975).

The conditioning operations emphasize formulating the appropriate response to the stimulus experience. These response operations include the following:

- identifying the structure of physiological response mechanisms (Deutsch and Deutsch, 1973; Hebb, 1949; Kimble, 1963; Rosenzweig and Bennett, 1976; Thompson, 1967);
- analyzing tasks or skills into elementary behavioral components (Calfee and Drum, 1978; Gagne, 1965; Gagne and Briggs, 1974; Mager, 1972);
- shaping behavioral responses from simple to complex (Skinner, 1969);
- actively formulating behavioral responses (Guthrie, 1952; Thorndike, 1931);
- actively reciting and practicing behavioral responses (Gates, 1917);
- reinforcing task-relevant behavioral responses (Meichenbaum and Asarnow, 1979; Wark, 1976; Watson and Tharp, 1977).

To sum, the contributions of the conditioning theories provide us with distinguishing dimensions of the stimulus

- **DISTINGUISHES STIMULUS DIMENSIONS**

- Distinguishing quantitatively and qualitatively

- Attaching discriminative cues

- Prescribing behavioral guidelines

- **FORMULATING APPROPRIATE RESPONSES**

- Identifying physiological mechanism

- Analyzing behavioral components

- Shaping behavioral responses

- Formulating behavioral responses

- Practicing behavioral responses

- Reinforcing task relevant responses

$$S \longrightarrow R$$

Figure 2–4. Conditioning Principles in S $\longrightarrow$ R Paradigm

and behavioral dimensions of the responses. Together, the conditioning patterns equip us with a response repertoire from which we may draw for reactive responses and upon which we may build for creative responses.

S $\longrightarrow$ O $\longrightarrow$ R Learning

The contributions of the S $\longrightarrow$ O $\longrightarrow$ R learning theories are momentous in terms of understanding the human organism as an intervening organizer. These concepts of learning treat the learner as a thinking, feeling and behaving organism with a history of learning experiences. Many of the learning operations have direct translations into teaching practices (Bower and Hilgard, 1981; Bugelski, 1979).

The contribution of S $\longrightarrow$ O $\longrightarrow$ R learning toward human processing revolves around the learners themselves (see Figure 2-5). As can be seen, the learning operations emphasize relating the learners' perceptions to the stimulus experience they are processing and the response they are formulating. Thus, the following operations of learning are offered:

- perceptually structuring tasks to highlight the learning (Kohler, 1925; Koffka, 1935; Wertheimer, 1959);
- systematically reducing learning and testing anxieties (Meichenbaum, 1977; Osterhouse, 1976; Wolpe, 1958);
- linking learner interests and learning goals (Goodwin and Coates, 1976);
- teaching for understanding of rules or principles (Katona, 1940);
- managing the classroom in order to foster learning (Lepper and Green, 1978; Mayer and Butterworth, 1979; O'Leary and O'Leary, 1972; Packard, 1970);
- reinforcing learning with numerous devices or learning aids (Atkinson, 1975; Bower, 1960; Furst, 1958; Lorayne and Lucas, 1974).

- **RELATION TO LEARNER PERCEPTIONS**
  - Perceptually structuring tasks
  - Reducing learning anxieties
  - Linking interests and goals
  - Teaching for understanding
  - Managing learning environment
  - Reinforcing with learning aids

- **FORMULATING APPROPRIATE RESPONSE**

- **DISTINGUISHING STIMULUS DIMENSIONS**

$$S \longrightarrow O \longrightarrow R$$

Figure 2-5. Learning Principles in S $\longrightarrow$ O $\longrightarrow$ R Paradigm

To sum, the contributions of the **S ⟶ O ⟶ R** learning approaches provide us with a greater understanding of the perceiving and organizing organism that intervenes between the stimulus and response. Moreover, they provide us with a base upon which to build a more comprehensive processing approach to the content of the Information Age.

S ⟶ P ⟶ R Processing

The contributions of human processing toward human development and achievement are profound. Human processing treats the human as the possessor of the most powerful instrument in the world: the brain. It is a brain that possesses all the intellectual power of the history of humankind and all the intellectual power in our existential universe. This brain enables us to envision things we have never seen and to go places we have never been.

The operations of human processing are built upon **S ⟶ R** and **S ⟶ O ⟶ R** approaches. The highly systematic operations in conjunction with the comprehensiveness of the dimensions distinguish **S ⟶ P ⟶ R** from the other approaches. However, the prepotent differentiating factors revolve around the ability of humans to process proactively for their own productive purposes.

Like **S ⟶ O ⟶ R** learning, the contributions of **S ⟶ P ⟶ R** processing revolve around the processors (see Figure 2-6). As can be seen, the processing operations emphasize systematizing how people naturally tend to explore, understand and act upon human experience (Carkhuff, 1983; Carkhuff and Berenson, 1981, 1986):

- exploring inclusively all potential sources of effect in human experience;
- understanding exclusively the most productive goals;
- acting upon programs to achieve the goals.

In turn, human processing operations emphasize systematizing the dimensions of the stimulus input to be processed (Carkhuff, 1986);

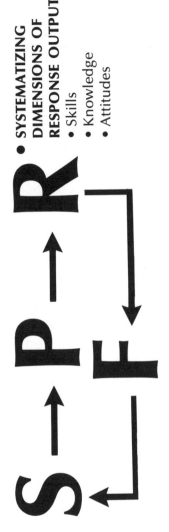

- **SYSTEMATIZING HUMAN PROCESSING**
  - Exploring human experience
  - Understanding human goals
  - Acting upon programs

- **SYSTEMATIZING DIMENSIONS OF RESPONSE OUTPUT**
  - Skills
  - Knowledge
  - Attitudes

- **SYSTEMATIZING DIMENSIONS OF STIMULUS**
  - Information
  - Person

- **SYSTEMATIZING FEEDBACK**
  - Productivity Information
  - Monitorizing and Management
  - Performance Improvement

Figure 2-6. Processing Principles in S ⟶ P ⟶ R Paradigm

- systematizing the information dimensions of the input;
- systematizing the personal dimension of the input.

All processing operations are, in turn, dedicated to systematizing performance dimensions of the response output (Carkhuff, 1983, 1984, 1986):

- systematizing skills;
- systematizing knowledge;
- systematizing attitudes.

Finally, processing operations are applied to systematizing feedback (Carkhuff, 1983, 1984, 1986):

- systematically feeding back productivity information;
- systematically implementing management programs;
- systematically implementing performance improvement programs.

Human processing systematically addresses all dimensions of all components of processing. It enables people to project into the future and to implement programs to achieve goals based upon those projections. It enables human processors to shape their own experiences as well as responses and, in so doing, to shape their own destinies.

In summary, the nature of human processing is critical both in terms of its strategies and their effects upon both the individual and the context. Until now, the individual was indeed conditionally determined. The conditioned responders and their more expansive counterparts, participative learners, were determined by the conditioning programs to which they were exposed. They were at worst dependent variables, and at best, interactive variables, in the determined equation of life.

Now comes the Age of Information with its overwhelming demands upon conditioned and participative responders. It presents humankind with the first human crisis since its origin: *whether or not to learn to process and, in so doing, for the first time in its 14-million-year history to become human.*

3.
Interpersonal Processing Through the Ages

In his capacity as director of HRD in the "Office of the Future" at IBM, Jack Kelly addressed what was a perennial problem of word processing and its relationship to office productivity. From his needs assessment, Kelly inferred that office productivity was determined by the level of interpersonal processing. For Kelly, interpersonal processing involved the interpersonal skills which enabled two or more people to share and resolve images of tasks to be performed. Without access to the office managers, he could approach only the other side of the productivity equation, the secretarial staff.

Assuming that secretaries utilized approximately 20–40% of word processing potential, he intervened to offer both substantive training in word processing and interpersonal processing skills. The trained secretaries were able to (1) facilitate their managers' development of the images of the tasks through their interpersonal skills, and (2) perform the word processing tasks at high levels. Kelly demonstrated significant improvements in the word processing task performance and significant reduction in problems encountered by the secretaries (Carkhuff, 1983, 1984). In other words, facilitated by the secretaries' interpersonal skills, the managers were able to make their objectives known more clearly. The managers experienced the secretaries' improvement as a function of their own managerial skills, and they took full credit for the improvement in office productivity.

29

The interdependency which characterizes the Information Age brings with it a responsibility for interpersonal processing. Interpersonal processing is unique in the history of humankind. It requires several behavioral skills: (1) that people process their responses intrapersonally before making contact; (2) that they share each other's images of the responses; (3) that they negotiate a merged image of the responses. All parties to the relationship are responsible for interpersonal processing skills.

For example, in living situations, peers, spouses, parents and children may process living problems or goals interpersonally. Each person explores, understands and acts to produce his or her image of the problem or goal; shares each other's images of the problems or goals; negotiates converged or merged images of problems or goals. Some may decide on a reasonable time for children to come home at night, others may organize responsibilities for housekeeping chores, and still others may develop plans for new housing.

Similarly, in learning situations like school or training, teachers and students may process learning problems or goals interpersonally. Teachers and students may process their images of learning problems or goals, share these images and negotiate merged images. They may decide upon instructional designs, learning objectives or teaching steps for resolving problems and achieving goals.

Working situations in the private or public sectors are identical. Employers and employees can process their images of work problems or goals in a similar manner. Problems or goals ranging from work tasks through management plans to labor relations may be defined, resolved or achieved.

In each instance, everyone involved has the responsibility to process individually before processing interpersonally. In order to do so, they'll need both individual processing skills and interpersonal processing skills. These skill requirements are different from all other ages of humankind. It is no longer enough simply to direct and control the other person's responses. Neither is it maximally productive for one person simply to facilitate the processing of the other. For the first time in the history of humankind, people must process interpersonally in order to produce interdependently (Carkhuff, 1969, 1983, 1984).

Directing and Controlling

The Industrial Era was characterized by conditioning. People were conditioned to respond to specific stimuli upon their presentation. They were assigned only the steps they needed to perform to complete a task. In other words, people were in a dependent role, depending upon others to assign the tasks.

For example, children were totally dependent upon parents, students upon teachers, and employees upon employers. One party directed and controlled the other. The other people simply received the directions and suffered the controls.

The implicit interpersonal formulations from psychoanalytic (Freud, 1924, 1933) and behavioristic (Watson, 1914) positions were attuned to the conditioning paradigm. Their promulgators postulated principles and designed programs for discriminating stimuli and controlling responses.

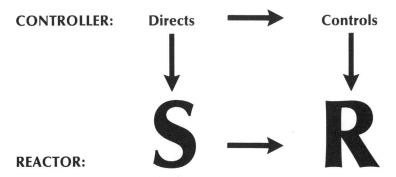

Figure 3–1. The Directing and Controlling Interpersonal Conditions of S ⟶ R Conditioning

31

We can view the stimulus ⟶ response (**S ⟶ R**) conditioning paradigm in Figure 3-1. As can be seen, the controlling person directs the delivery of the stimulus learning with experience and controls the action response evoked by the stimulus. In turn, the conditioned person makes the response conditioned to the stimulus. For example, teachers or employers present the stimulus directions or instructions for task or step performance. Students or employees make the appropriate response to the stimulus directions and the authority controls or reinforces the response.

The directing conditions of **S ⟶ R** conditioning served Industrial Era operatives well. For example, teachers and employers directed the activities of multiples of students or workers in the assembly-line version of the division of labor. Each person on the line performed only those few action steps or tasks required of him or her in a nonthinking or processing manner.

Facilitating Processing

It is paradoxical that only in the last 50 years of the history of humankind have people begun to look at interpersonal relations. Indeed, it is only with the advent of the Electronics Age (1960s to 1980s) that people institutionalized facilitating interpersonal relations. Instead of controlling other people's responses, facilitating interpersonal relations emphasized facilitating the other person's processing of responses.

The Electronics Era was influenced by the popular philosophies and interpersonal approaches of the neo-Freudians (Fromm, 1947; Horney, 1942; Sullivan, 1938) and the person-centered orientations (May, 1961; Rogers, 1951; Rogers and Dyamond, 1954). These positions argued for relating to the person's frame of reference, thus making all communications and learning instrumental for the individual's purposes.

The Electronics Era required an understanding of the response to be made. Thus, an organism intervened to understand the goals for responding. Instead of **S ⟶ R** conditioning, we conceive of this as **S ⟶ O ⟶ R** learning with the "O" representing the organizing and understanding organism.

For example, children may participate in setting their own goals for behavior and in determining alternative courses of action for achieving those goals before formulating an action response. Similarly, students may become involved in setting their own learning objectives before responding. Likewise, employees may participate in defining their performance tasks before implementing the steps of the tasks.

We can view the stimulus ⟶ organism ⟶ response **(S ⟶ O ⟶ R)** paradigm in Figure 3-2. As can be seen, the facilitating person responds to facilitate the learner's discrimination of the stimulus experience and the appropriate response. For example, both teachers and managers may provide the interpersonal conditions that facilitate students' and employees' processing of objectives, decision making and task performance.

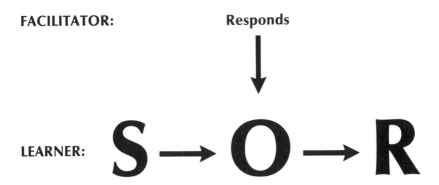

FACILITATOR: Responds

LEARNER: S ⟶ O ⟶ R

Figure 3-2. The Facilitating Interpersonal Conditions of S ⟶ O ⟶ R Learning

The facilitating conditions of **S** ➝ **O** ➝ **R** learning served the Electronics Era well. For example, teachers and managers interpreted and then shared information with workers. The students and workers participated in understanding the goals before making the action responses. Each person took responsibility for setting and defining goals before performing tasks.

Interdependent Processing

The extraordinary information "press" of the Information Age imposes a whole new set of requirements upon processing. The controllers simply cannot manage the information and the facilitators can no longer facilitate the processing by others. Instead of asking people to participate in understanding goals before acting, the Information Age provides entire data bases to all parties involved. Before getting together, all parties to a relationship are expected to process the entire data base. This means that all parties have explored the stimulus experience, understood the goals and acted upon the programs before sharing their images of their responses.

After the processors have processed individually, then they process interpersonally. This means that after each party has explored, understood and acted to formulate a response, they then come together to jointly formulate new responses. They accomplish this by sharing and negotiating new responses.

We can view the stimulus ➝ processing ➝ response (**S** ➝ **P** ➝ **R**) paradigm in Figure 3-3. As can be seen, after individual processing, the facilitator gets the other person's image of the response, gives his or her image of the response and negotiates a merger of the two responses. As can also be seen, more than one person may be involved in interdependent processing. For example, teachers and students or managers and employees may share images of a

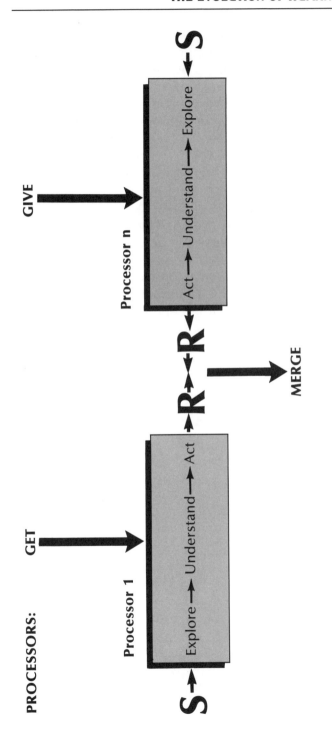

Figure 3-3. The Interdependent Conditions of S ⟶ P ⟶ R Processing

35

problem, negotiate merged images of the goals and plans to perform the tasks to achieve the goals.

The interdependent conditions of **S ⟶ P ⟶ R** learning are required by the Information Age. It is not enough that we process personally. We must also process interpersonally in order to close the gap between images of responses to be made and tasks to be performed. For example, students and workers as well as teachers and managers take responsibility for processing tasks. The managers alone can no longer handle the responsibility.

In summary, we can see the significance of this interdependent processing in our everyday lives. Parents', teachers' and employers' images can actually approximate the images or responses of their children, students and employees. Another word for this approximation of another person's responses is empathy. For example, each person must recognize the necessity for keeping the other "in business" as the assumption of interpersonal processing. In the Age of Information, *interdependency means that each person processes independently before sharing interdependently.* All individuals are dependent upon themselves and others to be productive.

4.
Organizational Processing Through the Ages

It is said that Peter Drucker, the noted industrial consultant, found his model for analyzing the industrial organization in the totalitarian organizations of his time (Drucker, 1939, 1942). As a young journalist in Nazi Germany, he studied the authoritarian structure of the Nazi government. Then in America he encountered the same hierarchical organization in General Motors and other corporate giants of the post-war era. At the top was "the Man." Below him were arranged, in increasing numbers, the traditional organizational pyramid: executives, managers or directors, supervisors of operations, production or delivery personnel. For its time, when information was slow to develop and circulate, the hierarchical organization worked. Every so often, new information was introduced and processed by "the Man" who handed down the tasks to be performed. But this model no longer works.

Most of the readers of this article have lived at least three decades. During that time, we have evolved from a rather primitive Industrial Age mentality through the complex digital and telecommunications operations of a transitional Electronics Era to the exciting information processing operations of the Information Age (Cyert and March, 1963; Drucker, 1954, 1974; Katz and Kahn, 1966; Likert, 1961; March and Simon, 1958; Thompson, 1967). Each age has been characterized developmentally and cumulatively by unique versions of processing: the Industrial Age by *mechanical* processing; the Electronics Era by *computer* processing; the Information Age by *human* processing.

Simultaneously, these ages have been characterized by the inputs and outputs that drove the periods: the raw materials that were transformed by mechanical processing into finished *products*; the information resources that were transformed by computer processing into consumer *services*; the human and information resources that were transformed by human processing into consumer *benefits*.

However, the critical ingredient of each age has been the mode of processing. Indeed, it has been both message and medium for its age. When we process mechanically, we make conditioned, nonthinking responses to produce products. When we process with the computer, we accelerate calculations to achieve our service goals. When we process as humans, we function interdependently to transform information into vital consumer benefits.

Just as human and interpersonal processing have evolved to meet the requirements of their ages, so does *organizational processing* respond to the demands being placed upon it by the various ages. To be sure, organizational processing incorporates the individual and interpersonal processing appropriate to its age. The organizational processing of the Industrial Age is based upon directing the stimulus input and controlling the response output. In turn, the organizational processing of the Electronics Era is dependent upon facilitating processing the stimulus input into response output. Also, the organizational processing of the Information Age emphasizes interpersonal sharing so that the response outputs of *independent processing* can be transformed into productive and merged responses. In effect, the response outputs of individuals are treated as stimulus inputs for interpersonal processing into productive responses.

The interdependency characterizing the Information Age requires interdependent processing. This type of processing emphasizes relationships between individuals and information as well as relationships between people. Indeed, people interrelate through their information outputs. Ultimately, *both* people and information grow through their synergistic interaction: as knowledge grows, human resources grow, and vice versa.

The key contributor to organizational processing is going to be the "critical mass" formed between individuals and information (Carkhuff, 1971; Carkhuff and Cannon, 1986). Models, designs or technologies generated by organizational personnel in interaction with their information base will determine their organization's productivity. For example, processing the *functions* rather than the *components* of the Qwerty keyboard in word processing produced a modification of the Dvorak keyboard that increased typists' productivity 60% to 80%. One such human processing breakthrough creates more productivity benefits than any amount of computerized performance monitoring over the employees' lifetime.

Mechanical Processing

The critical processing function in the Industrial Age was transforming natural resources from raw materials into finished products. The vehicle for implementing this transformation was mechanical processing.

These ingredients are reflected in the inputs, processes, outputs and feedback in organizational productivity systems during that time (see Figure 4-1). As can be seen, the primary inputs were raw materials and capital resources that financed the machinery purchases and labor. The processing was mechanical. The controls emphasized supervisory monitoring. The outputs were constituted by the finished products. Information regarding the results outputs was recycled as feedback to the system.

The key to processing in the Industrial Age was the machinery. Labor was seen only as a necessary extension of the machinery, to be supplanted over time by another piece

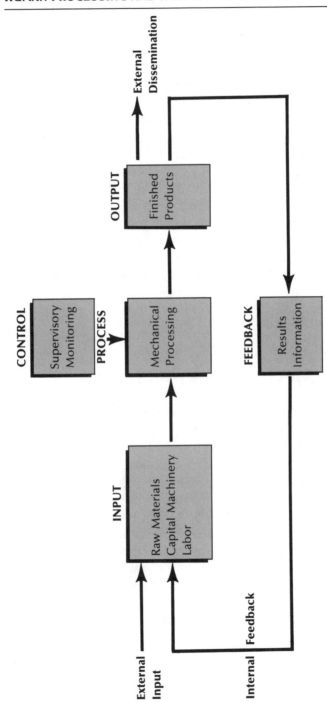

Figure 4–1. Organizational Processing in the Industrial Age

of machinery. Industrial psychologists reinforced this view of human resources by conducting time and motion studies to mechanize the machinery operators' role.

At the same time, interpersonal processing of any kind was minimized. The organization was structured in a pyramidal hierarchy. "The Man" was at the top. He had exclusive access to relatively constant information. He analyzed and synthesized the information before sharing goals with his managers. They, in turn, assigned mechanical processing tasks to uninformed, unthinking robot-like laborers.

To sum, organizational processing in the Industrial Age was predominantly mechanical. Individual processing was minimal. Human resources—in the form of labor—were seen as extensions of machinery. Interpersonal processing was absent as "the Man" defined and enforced his will.

Computer Processing

Computers dominated organizational processing in the Electronics Age. Basically, computers provided the "intelligence" for high technology machinery, which transformed natural resources into consumer products. In addition, the organizational processing transformed human and information resources into the consumer services attendant to the products.

As can be seen in Figure 4-2, the primary inputs were the capital resources used to purchase high-tech machinery, human and information resources. The computer serves to drive or complement mechanical processing. Products were wrapped "inside" services outputs as the economy moved toward becoming a service-oriented economy. The control function was discharged by participative management styles in which managers shared in the decision making about goals and courses of action. Feedback emphasized information on productivity comparing results outputs to resource inputs with an emphasis upon maximizing efficiency of investment.

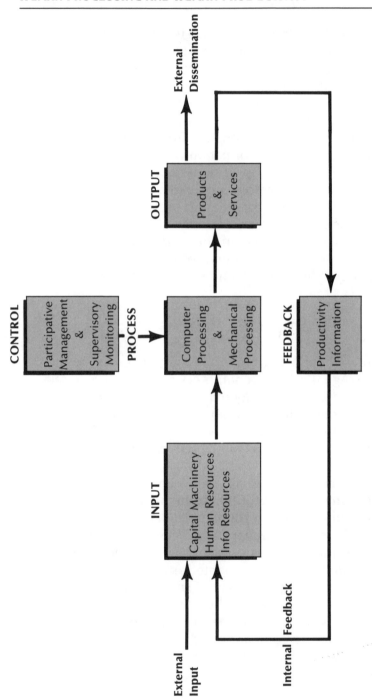

Figure 4-2. Organizational Processing in the Electronics Era

The key to processing in the Electronics Age was the computer. Somewhat paradoxically, human labor was elevated to be capable not only of operating the computer but also of creating configurations for systems and innovations in technology. Thus, participative management at the management levels and quality circles at the delivery or production levels were in vogue as upper levels of management searched to accomplish greater cost efficiencies.

In this context, interpersonal processing was introduced. Basically, one person—the manager or supervisor—facilitated the processing of others—the supervisees or delivery personnel. Usually, the processing involved expanding the quantity of responses available to the personnel through sharing. The processing was dedicated to maximizing resource efficiencies while maintaining results effectiveness.

To sum, organizational processing in the Electronics Era was computer-dominated. Interpersonal processing leading to response sharing was introduced as both managers and delivery personnel were increasingly involved in decision making at their respective levels of responsibility.

Human Processing

The great paradox of the Information Age is that as information emerged as a dominant resource input, human processing emerged as the dominant processing vehicle. The reason was simple: the press of information was so extraordinary that it demanded instantaneous processing.

As can be seen in Figure 4-3, the critical inputs are human and information resources complemented by the capital resources needed to purchase the computer and high-tech machinery. Human processing dominates even while the computers and high-tech machinery are being elevated in quality and power. Products and services culminate in consumer benefit outputs. Controls are eliminated as both consumer and producer productivity information is fed back for purposes of recycling processing and self-management.

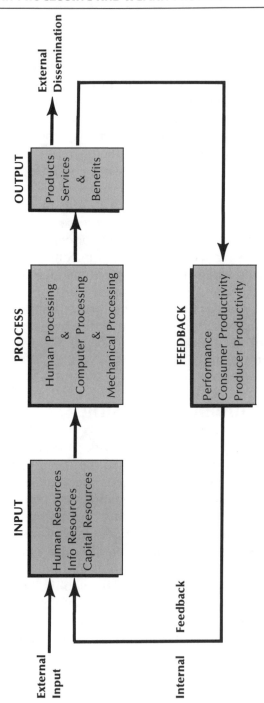

Figure 4–3. Organizational Processing in the Age of Information

Clearly, the key to processing in the Information Age is people. In interaction with information resources, the human processor forms a "critical mass" of processing. Together, human and information resources upgrade each other, producing innovations in models, systems and technologies that maximize productivity. Relatedly, interpersonal processing emphasizes interdependent processing in which each party to the relationship accomplishes the following activities: processing individually, interpersonally and interdependently.

In conclusion, organizational processing in the Information Age is dominated by humans who are complemented by computers. Human processing emphasizes individual processing before interpersonal and interdependent processing as the critical sources of maximizing human productivity.

All organizational processing is dedicated to human productivity. Human productivity may be defined as follows: *human processing for human purposes*. A human productivity system is initiated by human and information resource inputs. It is implemented in the synergistic interaction of human and information resources: each contributes to the development of the other. It culminates in outputs that are beneficial to the producer and the consumer: the consumer's productivity is enhanced by more productive products and services; the producer's productivity is also enhanced in terms of more productive human and information resources.

To understand the human productivity system, it is helpful to understand what it is *not*. It is not the quality control or supervisory monitoring practices grown out of the Industrial Age. It is not a participative management system that seeks to engage people in designing their own demise; nor is it a micro-management system that seeks to use the computer to drain the last few drops of performance out of an Industrial Age mentality.

The human is both the means and the ends of organizational processing. The human processes in order to produce benefits that the human receives. Nowhere can we see the ethic more clearly than in the concept of consumer productivity. The human productivity system exists first and foremost to help make the consumer more productive, i.e., to reduce consumer resource inputs while increasing results outputs. The human productivity system exists secondarily only to help make the producer more productive. It is only after the producer has been effective in facilitating consumer productivity that the producer becomes efficient in achieving producer productivity.

Organizational processing emphasizes human processing for human productivity. The central ingredient in human productivity is consumer productivity. *The goal of organizational processing is to help the consumer in business by maximizing their results outputs while minimizing their resource inputs.* At its core, human productivity is an ethical system that serves to expand the universe of options for the consumer.

III.
Toward Models for
Human Processing

5.
Individual Processing in the Age of Information

We can see the prototype of human processing in the first year of a child's life. The child learns to explore, understand and act upon his or her world. What goes on during this first year of life continues in more and more refined ways throughout our lives—or not! How productively we live our lives depends totally upon how effectively and efficiently we learn to process.

A great deal depends upon how we develop our human resources. For example, it depends upon how the environment—which is largely human—interacts with our biological selves. The newborn infant enters the world with few skills other than physiological reflex responses. For example, the child has the sucking and the palmar or grasping reflex.

If the environment is responsive to the child, these reflexes will become instrumental in the child's survival. They constitute the child's initial movements toward the world which will ultimately lead to his or her growth and development. The child will be able to nurse with the sucking reflex. Later on, the child will be able to manipulate things with the grasping reflex.

In the beginning, however, newborn infants bring little but their inherent resources to their worlds. In their utter dependency, they wait for us to insure their survival by responding to their needs, and by gradually guiding them to the things they need to have to maintain themselves.

One of the ways that we guide our children is by helping them to form habits. Basically, human habits are behaviors that are acquired without human intelligence. They can be acquired by associating or relating, in space and time, two or more sets of activities. At least one of these activities must satisfy some human need in order for the behavior to be repeated as a habit. For example, the child may develop the sucking habit when nourished by the mother's breast. The results may be said to be instrumental in satisfying the child's need for nourishment.

In the process, the child may develop a "conditioned" sucking response to the stimulus of the mother's nipple. In a similar manner, the child may later on develop a conditioned grasping response to the stimulus of food, which is instrumental in satisfying the child's need for nourishment. There are many other kinds of life habits which can be developed without human intelligence or intentionality. The habits are "learned" only in the sense that they are repeated. They are not learned in the sense of being the product of human understanding. In fact, these habits are conditioned, spinal responses, not processed responses.

Human learning and, indeed, human intelligence begin to manifest themselves when children are several months old. At this point, children begin to explore themselves and their environment. They discover the existence of and the relationships between environmental stimuli and their own responses. In other words, children become aware of the association of **stimuli** to which they have become conditioned to and the **responses** which have been conditioned to the stimuli. They become aware of causes and effects in their worlds.

This awareness is a two-way street. For example, children become aware that the nipple or the food serves as stimulus to a sucking or grasping response. This response, in turn, will lead to satisfying a need for nourishment. Children may then become aware that a need for nourishment stimulates the response of search for the nipple or the food.

Through exploring, children become aware of both their past and present relationships to their environments—

including themselves. Children attempt to describe where they are in relation to themselves and the worlds around them. **Exploring** is the first stage or phase of human learning. This form of exploration begins to distinguish humankind from all other forms of life.

It is a short step from becoming aware of the ingredients of human experience to anticipating experiences. With increasing confidence in this awareness of the relationship of stimulus and response, children are prepared for instrumental or purposeful learning at about one year of age. In other words, children set out to obtain certain results or ends. For example, children may set out to attract their mother, or to obtain food or an object that is out of reach.

Drawing from this awareness of the relationship between stimulus and response or cause and effect, children set goals of achieving certain effects. The goals of the instrumental act are often only seen later although some approximation of them was obviously intended from the beginning.

In short, children understand their relationships to future events or experiences. They are attempting to predict the consequences of their efforts. They understand where they want to be in their worlds. This **understanding** is the second stage or phase of human learning. It is what allows humankind to anticipate its future—which further distinguishes us from other forms of life.

The next phase of human learning flows naturally from the understanding phase. It involves the development of behavioral patterns instrumental to achieving goals. From the end of the first year onward, children draw from their repertoire of behaviors to produce the responses needed to achieve a goal. For example, children may laugh or cry to bring their caretakers to them. Children may move their hands in the direction of unreachable food or objects. There may be a series of trial and error experiences. These experiences may either confirm the child's responses because the goal is reached and they've experienced satisfaction, or else the experiences may deny the child's responses because the goal is not reached.

Children begin to act in order to get from where they are to where they want to be within their worlds. They are attempting to control themselves and their worlds. **Acting** *is the third stage or phase of learning. It enables human beings to plan and work toward the end of influencing their future.*

Human Processing

The first year of human development serves as a prototype for all human processing. Children's reflexes are unknowingly conditioned as habitual responses to certain stimuli. These habits serve as the limited repertoire of responses with which children initially approach the world. Improvement in the quantity and quality of responses with which the learner ultimately relates to the world depends upon the development of the children's intelligence. This, in turn, depends upon how effectively they go through the stages or phases of learning.

Initially, children *explore* and identify the nature of the stimuli and responses in their experience. Then, children come to *understand* the interactive nature of stimuli and responses, anticipate the effects of one upon the other and develop goals to achieve these effects. Finally, children *act* by drawing from their developing repertoire of responses to attempt to achieve goals. The children's action behavior is shaped by feedback or by the effects it achieves. This feedback is recycled as input through the stages or phases of learning as the children explore more extensively, understand more accurately, and act more effectively. This ascending, enlarging spiral of exploration, understanding and action is the source of the adult's improving repertoire of responses.

It is important to note that as learners develop, they may process differently depending upon their own learning styles and functions. For example, some learners may *begin* with an action response which they later explore and understand. Nevertheless, the exploring-understanding-acting sequence may be cycled to produce more effective and efficient action responses.

The Skills of Exploring

Just watch the learners' exploratory activities in school. Perhaps we can see these in a classroom most clearly when there is an absence of formal teaching. The learners may become interested in some object or mechanism, on their own initiative, in the absence of a teacher. The learners will approach the material or object and position themselves so as to give it their attention. They may observe it for a while, perhaps listen to it and then probably touch it. The touching will lead to handling. The learners may try this out in different ways, turning the material around or over, or attaching it to other things.

The learners may try to figure out what the thing is and does, and maybe even why and how it does it. Finally, they may try to do whatever it does. In the process, they have found out what they know about it, and what they can do with it. In short, they have found out where they are in relation to the learning experience. (So have their teachers, if they are present.)

The learners must address all sources of learning in a similar manner. If the teacher is presenting content in the classroom, the learners must use all of their exploring skills to address the teacher, the content, the delivery or method, and the classroom environment as dimensions of the learning experience. Learners must also address themselves as potential sources of learning, in terms of the learning experiences and learning skills that they bring to the learning process. By exploring all dimensions of the learning experience, the learners can find out *where they are* in relation to the learning experience. They will then be ready to find out *where they want to be.*

The Skills of Understanding

The learners may engage in a series of understanding activities. They may relate the dimensions of their current experiences to those of their past. They may organize the dimensions of these experiences in different ways based upon their similarities and differences. The learners may organize the dimensions of the learning experience in still different ways based upon their functions and the values of these functions to their learning. The learners may generalize their needs for these values and set generalized learning goals based upon the learning experience and specific learning objectives derived from the different dimensions of the learning experience. Or they may do all of this by simply determining what, of all the content possible, they have yet to learn.

Where there is a teacher with a teaching goal, all of these activities can take place in relation to that goal: the learners may set their learning objectives in relation to the teaching goals. Where there is no teacher, the learners may set their learning objectives based upon their generalized needs. In other words, the learners gain increasing confidence in their understanding of where they are in relation to where they want to be. They are ready to act in order to get there.

The Skills of Acting

Observing the learners in the action phase reveals the types of activities in which learners engage. First, they work to master the knowledge and skills involved in the learning goals. If the teachers have established the goal, they learn the knowledge or skills the teachers have developed. If teachers are not involved, learners can begin to define their skills objectives in terms of the deficits or problems they are having in achieving their goals, and to develop and implement programs designed to achieve those objectives.

In either event, having acquired the learning, the learners can repeat or practice the skill involved until it is ready and effectively available to them. Then they can apply it, either in some way that was intended by the teacher, or that is relevant to their own experience. They can continue to apply it in real life, everyday living, learning, playing and working experiences. Finally, they can transfer the learning to unique and creative situations in their lives. This is the culmination of mastery: to be able to use what you have learned to create.

The Phases of Human Processing

People in the everyday world process their experience in a similar manner. They process the information about people, data and things they receive as input. They explore, understand and act in order to transform these stimulus inputs into productive response outputs.

For example, parents in a living environment may explore, understand and act upon their children's behavior, information regarding their mortgage, or the installation of new equipment. Youth may process parents' or peers' values, information on their school or course options and instructions regarding use of a personal computer.

Similarly, teachers in a learning environment may process student's learning behavior, data regarding student's learning performance and information regarding the use of a new computerized data system. In turn, the learners may process information regarding peoples of other cultures, data regarding their own aptitudes and abilities, and learn to manage to manipulate the two extraordinary instruments of our time—the automobile and the computer. In this context, the compatability of teacher and learner objectives is critical. *The productive teacher accommodates the learners' functional objectives* instead of allowing the learners to merely adjust to the teacher's processes.

Processing in the work setting is similar. Policymakers and managers process primarily information on people or data while supervisors, delivery and production personnel process raw materials into finished products, raw data into useful information and naive candidates into productive workers. In the working context, unlike the teaching/

learning context, productive delivery personnel must incorporate the goals and objectives of their managers and supervisors in implementing their tasks. However, increasingly in the high tech and knowledge businesses, the tasks are shared and then merged interdependently. Over time, the middle and lower levels of management will disappear, as delivery personnel process all aspects of data with the purpose of improving self-management and performance.

What these people in all of these settings have in common is *processing*. They *explore* the stimulus experience in order to know where they are in relation to it. They *understand* where they are in relation to where they want or need to be with their experience. They *act* to get from where they are to where they want or need to be.

However, it is important to emphasize that not all processing is dedicated to specific living, learning or working purposes. Often the objectives are defined and programs developed only to be able to communicate them. The purposes may not be clear at the moment, but the information may be stored for future use.

For example, in science and other intellectual pursuits, we are frequently communicating objectives without specific or immediate purposes. However, parents may also communicate objectives to their children, teachers to learners, and managers to employees for purposes of future reference. In reading this book, for example, the processor will learn to store operationally defined objectives which they will retrieve on demand in the future.

The Human Processing Model

The model of human processing revolves around the ingredients of the basic individual processing system: stimulus, processing, response and feedback (see Figure 5-1). Basically, we (1) systematize the dimensions of the stimulus input so that we (2) can systematically process it into (3) productive response output and (4) feedback productivity

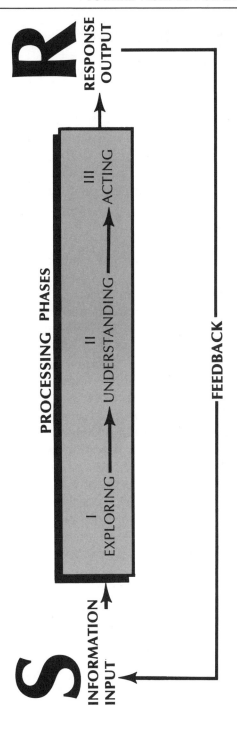

Figure 5-1. The Phases of Human Processing

information in order to make the future responses still more productive.

Stimulus Input

The first ingredient in the processing model emphasizes the dimensions of the stimulus input. There are basically two dimensions: information and personal. Actually, the critical dimensions of stimulus input move from person to information to person.

In this context, the information factor is comprised of both (1) the personal values that lead us to search out certain information and (2) the content of that information. The values are simply intentions the processor is seeking to fulfill or satisfy. The content is comprised of the components of knowledge—facts, concepts and principles.

Relatedly, the personal factor is comprised of both personal and intrapersonal dimensions. The personal dimensions consider the implications of information for the person. The intrapersonal dimensions emphasize the experience of the person who is processing.

The values provide a reason for processing. They enable us to factor or isolate that information which is productive for our purposes. For example, in parenting, we may be able to look at the living values of both parents and children. In teaching, we may be able to look at the learning values of both teachers and learners. Also, in employment, we may have the working values of both employers and employees. These values will undergo change as they are defined in productivity terms and as productivity policy to guide decision making.

The content of the information, then, is factored in terms of the values with which an individual approaches input. The content consists of the knowledge and operations that produce behavior relevant to the values. For example, it may have to do with knowledge or skills in parenting, teaching or learning or working. Just as the values do, the content undergoes change as it is analyzed, synthesized and operationalized to produce productive information.

The personal dimension refers to the requirements of the processing of content. The requirements may apply to the processors themselves, or they may apply to personnel upon whom the processing is focused. Personal information involves personal implications for the skills, knowledge and attitudes required by both the processing of content and the content itself. For example, teachers or trainers may lack the teaching skills, knowledge or attitudes required by the teaching or learning content. Personal information also changes with the focus of the operation during exploring, understanding and acting.

The intrapersonal dimension of information refers to the experience of processing. When the processor personalizes his or her own experience, we may think of this as *intrapersonal processing*. When someone else, a facilitator, serves to personalize the processing, we may think of this as *interpersonal processing*. In effect, the processor or the facilitator individualizes the experience of processing. For example, the teachers or trainers may feel good/bad about the values they are satisfying or good/bad about the requirements that are imposed upon them by the processing of content. The intrapersonal dimension also changes with the other dimensions throughout the course of processing.

Human Processing

The second ingredient, then, is human processing itself. Processing is accounted for by three primary phases: *exploring* human experience; *understanding* human goals; *acting* upon programs to achieve the goals (Carkhuff, 1983, 1984, 1986; Carkhuff and Berenson, 1981).

Exploring emphasizes discovering where we are in relation to the input we are receiving. We may explore where we are in relation to information or person. In relation to information, we may define our values or analyze content.

In relation to people, we may diagnose ourselves or respond to our experience. For example, job candidates may
explore where they are in relation to career values and
career information. Likewise, they may consider the personal implications as well as the experience of exploring
information.

Understanding emphasizes knowing where we are in relation to where we want or need to be. Again, we may understand our goals in relation to information or person. Thus,
we can define new, more productive values and synthesize
content into goal statements. On the other hand, we can
set and personalize goals. For example, job candidates may
understand career goals by making career decisions based
upon values and synthesizing content into guiding principles or goal statements. In a similar manner, they may
consider the personal implications and the experience of
their understanding of goals.

Acting emphasizes developing and acting upon programs
to get from where we are to where we want or need to be.
Again, we can act upon information by developing policy or
defining objectives. Likewise, we can act personally by
developing and acting upon programs. For example, job
candidates may develop career plans and act to take the
necessary steps to conduct job interviews.

Response Output

The third ingredient in the processing model, then, emphasizes the *dimensions of the response output*. The critical
variance of the response output is accounted for by three
dimensions: the skills, the knowledge, and the attitudes required to make a productive response.

Skills may be seen in the mechanics of performance.
Skills are defined by the operations, conditions, and stan-
dards of task implementation: What is it? What does it do?
How does it do it? Where and when? How well? For example, a job-seeking candidate may require career decision

making or job interviewing skills in order to choose a productive course of action or make a productive response.

Knowledge has to do with the factual data and conceptual formulations required of the individual. Basically, knowledge is an inference from performance that tells us the performer knows the facts, concepts, and principles involved. For example, a job-seeking candidate may require factual data on the job marketplace, conceptual knowledge concerning the use of career information, and career development principles that guide his or her movement through the marketplace.

Finally, attitudes can be inferred from the intensity and endurance of performance. Sharply focused responses and ongoing iterations of improving response imply the motivation to produce. Similarly, accurately formulated responses and ongoing exchanges intended to improve performance imply interdependent concerns and interpersonal relations. For example, productive motivational attitudes may be inferred from productive interpersonal response in the job interview or on the job with peers and subordinates as well as superiors.

Feedback

The processing is not complete until feedback is provided to the processor. Basically, feedback is recycled as input. It revolves around productivity information, self-monitoring and self-management (Carkhuff, 1983, 1984, 1986; Carkhuff and Cannon, 1986).

The productivity information is simply a message concerning the effectiveness and efficiency of the response. It is recycled to the processor so they can improve their future responses. For example, the job seeker may need to emphasize responding to the interviewer's experience rather than initiating from his or her own experience in the job interview.

The immediate purpose of feedback is to enable processors to monitor and, as a result, manage themselves.

Monitoring milestones, timelines and evaluations of task performance tell the processor whether he or she has performed the task on time and at a high level of productivity. This self-monitoring provides the feedback necessary to modify self-management planning and implementation functions.

The longer-range purpose of the feedback is performance improvement. The feedback serves to recycle the processing: more extensive exploring, more accurate understanding, more productive acting. The improved processing serves to improve the productivity of the response as feedback is recycled once again.

The Skills of Human Processing

Stimulus input may be processed into productive information which, when acted upon, may constitute response output. Clearly, the human processing activities are the critical ingredients in transforming raw data into productive information. These processing activities may be enacted in linear, parallel, sequential and interactive fashion.

We can see the values dimension processed through the phases of processing in Figure 5-2. As can be seen, personal

PHASES OF PROCESSING

EXPLORING ⟶ UNDERSTANDING ⟶ ACTING

EXPLORING	UNDERSTANDING	ACTING
Defining	Defining	Defining
Personal	Productivity	Productivity
Values	Values	Policy

Figure 5-2. Values Processing Skills

values are defined in order to explore where we are; the values are defined in productivity terms (recycling resource investments while increasing results benefits) in order to understand where we want or need to be; the values are transformed into productivity policy in order to act to make decisions and achieve our goals.

For example, in reading this material, you may define your values in terms of investing an hour of your time and resources in accomplishing an awareness of the content of thinking (*Exploring*). Later on, you may wish to define your values more productively in terms of learning the skills for thinking in return for your investment (*Understanding*). After this, you may develop your own policy to define your own mission of learning and teaching thinking skills (*Acting*).

We can view the content dimension in the phases of processing (see Figure 5-3). Here the content of facts, concepts and principles is analyzed in order to explore where we are. Then, the content is synthesized in order to understand where we want or need to be. Finally, the content is operationally defined in order to act to get there.

PHASES OF PROCESSING

EXPLORING ⟶ UNDERSTANDING ⟶ ACTING

Analyzing
Content

Synthesizing
Content

Operationalizing
Content

Figure 5-3. Content Processing Skills

For example, in processing the content you are reading, you may analyze the knowledge I am presenting to you and formulate an operating principle for where you are:

If people process by thinking (rather than conditioning), then they will be able to achieve their goals.

Further, you may synthesize a new and more productive principle for where you want or need to be:

If people process by productive thinking skills, then they will be able to achieve their goals more productively.

Finally, you may operationalize an objective for acting to acquire productive thinking skills:

The learners/teachers/managers will learn to think productively by exploring, understanding and acting in school/work during school/work hours and at levels of skill application and transfer.

The objective is defined in achievable terms.

Similarly, we may view the personal implications of processing information (see Figure 5-4). During exploring, a person diagnoses where he or she is in relation to the skills, knowledge and attitudinal requirements of the content. During understanding, the person sets personal goals for developing the required skills, knowledge and attitudes. Finally, during acting, the person develops programs in order to act to achieve these goals.

PHASES OF PROCESSING

EXPLORING $\longrightarrow$	UNDERSTANDING $\longrightarrow$	ACTING
Diagnosing Personal Functioning	Setting Personal Goals	Developing Personal Programs

Figure 5–4. Personal Processing Skills

For example, in processing the personal implications of this book, you may diagnose your own functioning: Do I have the productive thinking skills, knowledge and attitudes? Further, you may set personal goals for your own functioning: I want or need to have individual processing or productive thinking skills, knowledge and attitudes. Or you may develop programs to achieve the desired PTS skills, knowledge and attitudes.

Finally, we may view the phases of intrapersonal processing (see Figure 5-5). During exploring, the person responds to experience in order to know where he or she is. During understanding, the person personalizes goals in order to discover where he or she wants or needs to be. During acting, the person initiates action programs in order to get to the goals.

For example, in processing the intrapersonal experience, you may respond to your own experience of exploring:

"I feel conflicted about programs for thinking."

Further, you may personalize your goals for learning:

"I feel disappointed because I do not have thinking skills and am eager to learn productive thinking skills."

Finally, you may initiate individualized action steps for learning:

PHASES OF PROCESSING

EXPLORING ⟶ UNDERSTANDING ⟶ ACTING

Responding   Personalizing   Initiating
to Experience   Goals   Programs

Figure 5–5. Intrapersonal Processing Skills

"My goal is to learn productive thinking skills."
"My program involves learning exploring, understanding and acting.
"My first step is to prepare physically, emotionally and intellectually for learning."
You are now ready to learn PTS.

The Systems of Human Processing

These dimensions and phases of information may be put together in different systems. For example, they may be processed in a linear and sequential manner as exhibited in Figure 5-6. As can be seen, the *values* are processed into *policy* before the *content* is processed into *objectives*. Then, the objectives are cycled through personal processing into programs and the programs through intrapersonal processing into action steps.

Typically, most people process in a linear fashion. Thus, they focus upon one or another dimension, often to the exclusion of others. For example, some of you may or may not have been looking for something which you do not find in this book. This will impact your values. Others may process the book, regardless of their values.

Another way of processing—perhaps more familiar to us—involves sequential processing. Here values and content are processed simultaneously before processing personally and intrapersonally (see Figure 5-7). As can be seen, the dimensions of information are processed before the person dimensions are processed.

This processing is familiar to those of us in teaching and training. We may employ our values to develop our content. Then, in learning-to-teach, we may consider the personal implications and intrapersonal experience for us as teachers. Similarly, in learning-to-learn, our learners may process the personal and intrapersonal dimensions of the content which we have developed and delivered to them. In the case of this book, we processed the information

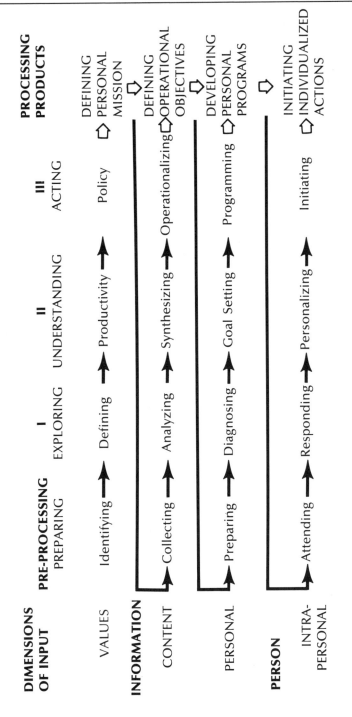

Figure 5-6. An Illustration of Linear and Sequential Human Processing

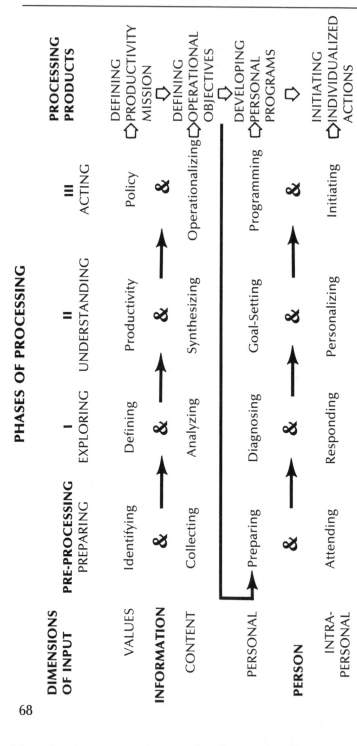

Figure 5–7. An Illustration of Simultaneous and Sequential Human Processing

before presenting it to you. You may process the personal implications of the requirements imposed upon you, and the intrapersonal experience of your feelings about the processing.

Finally, the human processing model may also be seen in a comprehensive, interactive mode (see Figure 5-8). It is possible that the dimensions are processed interactively within and between the phases of processing. Indeed, in keeping with the enormous power of the human brain, the dimensions may be processed simultaneously and interactively.

Thus, in comprehensive processing, during the preparation phase the person may prepare the information by identifying goal areas which guide the collection of information. Simultaneously, the person prepares personally for processing and attends to the experience of the processor.

During the exploring phase, the processor may explore the information simultaneously as follows: defining the values which guide the search for the content to be analyzed; considering the personal implications of the analysis of the content; and responding to the processor's exploring of experience.

During the understanding phase, the processor may understand the information simultaneously as follows: defining the productivity values which enable the individualizing necessary to synthesize the content; considering the personal implications of the synthesis of the content; and personalizing the processor's understanding of goals.

Finally, during the acting phase, the processor may act upon the information simultaneously as follows: developing the policy which guides the selection of the objective to be operationally defined; considering the personal implications for programs to achieve the operational objectives; and initiating the actions based upon the programs.

Again, the values processing produces guiding policy or missions while the content processing concludes in operational definitions of the objectives. The personal and intrapersonal processing produces personal programs which culminate in acting to perform responses.

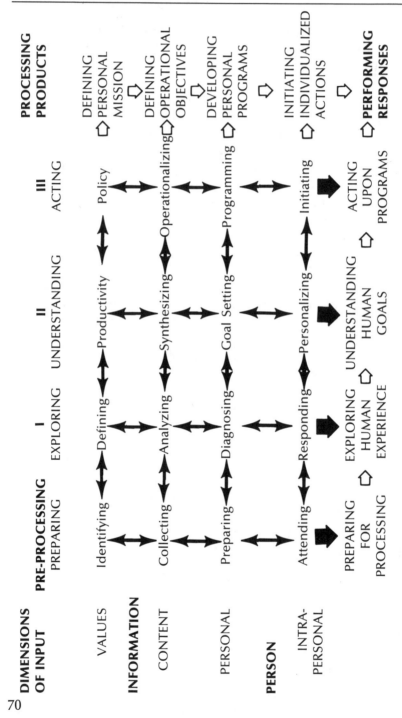

Figure 5-8. An Illustration of Comprehensive Interactive Human Processing

For example, the head of any family, classroom or school, public or private sector organization may seek to develop a mission and policy in a given area. The person may prepare for processing by collecting and organizing information about the appropriate goal areas. In processing, this policy maker explores, understands and acts upon his or her values, the content of the information processed and the personal implications of the processing. The processor would then perform a series of responses comprised of the skills, knowledge and attitudes developed and applied. These responses would produce the policy products, the guidelines that service the recipients, and produce the potential consumer benefits. The productivity of both the performer/producer and the consumer would be assessed and its information product fed back to improve the responses.

In a similar manner, the children in a family, the students in school, or the employees in an organization would process the input of the policy statement: preparing by collecting, organizing and personal preparation; processing by exploring, understanding and acting; performing responses with skills, knowledge and attitudes; producing their own products, services and benefits; assessing response performance and consumer and producer productivity; feedbacking productivity information; improving responses.

We can view individual processing in the Age of Information from another perspective (see Figure 5-9). As can be seen, the stimulus inputs are converted into response outputs by processing the informational and personal dimensions through the phases of processing: exploring, understanding, acting.

The important thing to remember about human processing is that it is the most effective and efficient way to become productive. While learning processing skills may seem complex and cumbersome at times, in fact, the entire process will take place in fractions of a second. Of necessity, the learning must be sequential and detailed. In practice, the dimensions of processing are often simultaneous

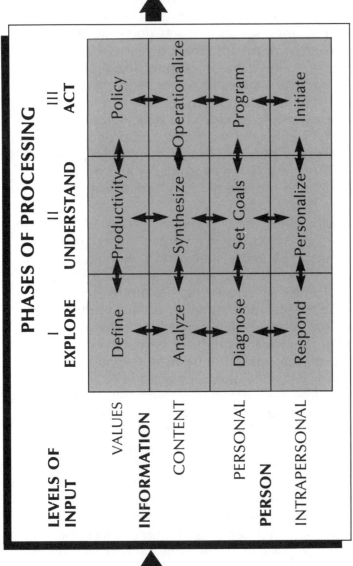

Figure 5-9. Individual Processing in the Age of Information

and interactive. Learning processing is like learning any complex skill. At first, it seems cognitive and sequential. Ultimately, as it accommodates the instantaneous power of the brain, it is automatic and fluid.

The implications for humans are clear. Not only must individuals be completely open to receiving information, but they must also *actively elicit updated and accurate information* relevant to their areas of functioning. Further, they must learn to process and recycle their processing at higher and higher levels. They must direct this processing to productivity values and feedback the productivity information for purposes of self-management.

The institutional implications are also clear. Homes and parents must be interfaced with schools and teachers in order to deliver higher-level human resources to the schools. In turn, schools and teachers must interact with businesses in order to deliver higher-level human resources to business and industry. Each setting must emphasize teaching, supporting and reinforcing the acquisition, application and transfer of individual processing skills.

In summary, human processing skills merge human values and thinking skills in a highly contingent human processing model. The human processing model provides a cognitive map for the phases of human processing: preparing to process the stimulus input; processing by exploring, understanding and acting upon the input; performing the response and producing products, services and benefits; assessing, feedbacking and improving the performance and productivity of the response. In this context, it is important to view feedback on past responses and products as part of the input to be processed anew. Feedback contributes to increasing the variance of input along with external input. Together, internal feedback and external input enable the processing of a new and more productive response. Just as the processors require cognitive maps detailing their destinations, so do the readers of this material require cognitive maps detailing the models and systems of human processing and human productivity.

6.
Interpersonal Processing in the Age of Information

Typically, managers and supervisors spend approximately 50% of their time in crises management. That is to say, the delivery or production-line personnel have performed their tasks incorrectly, produced inadequate products, or provided insufficient services. The source of these crises is the old "Give and Go" tradition of industry: the bosses **give** the orders and the employees **go** out and implement them. The problem with the "Give and Go" system is that there is no clear agreement on the task to be performed. Often, the supervisor lacks specific details of the operations. Usually, the employee has little or no opportunity to offer either input to or feedback on the assignment.

It may be argued, as it has been by many managers and supervisors, that the "Give and Go" approach is extremely efficient. This approach usually involves, at most, a few minutes of ordering people around. There is often no response from the employee nor, so far as the manager is concerned, any need for one.

One area of a new multi-phased management program implemented at General Dynamics Corporation involved specific modification of the traditional "Give and Go" pattern. This area of the new program involved a great deal more time for managers and supervisors. They had to "Get, Give, Merge and Go." This required them to **get** the employees' images of the task, **give** or share their own *images, negotiate a* **merger** *or convergence of the images of the goal if there were discrepancies, and work with the employees to develop a program. The employees would then* **go** *out and implement the program to achieve the goal. Sometimes this process would take ten or even twenty minutes, especially where there were critical discrepancies in images. Nevertheless, upon mandate from above, the managers and supervisors obediently followed orders and entered interpersonal training. What happened next was a surprise to them.*

They became involved in the training process and received the content readily. Moreover, they acquired the skills involved and were able to apply them to training objectives in the exercises.

More important, follow-up studies indicated that the managers and supervisors were able to apply their skills to their tasks at work. They were pleased to discover the skills were applicable at home with their families and in the community with friends. Further, they found the skills could be transferred to their other learning experiences, both formal and informal.

Perhaps most important for our purposes, these personnel found that when they made the front-end investment of sharing and converging images of tasks, they received the concomitant benefits of improved performance. Under the old "Give and Go" orders, crises often grew steadily and cumulatively because of gaps in employee and/or managerial understanding of specific tasks. Under the "Get, Give, Merge and Go" program, the managers found that they were preventatively reducing or eliminating crises because both they and the employees understood the tasks.

Just as the different ages of humankind require different individual processing strategies, so do they also require different interpersonal processing strategies (Carkhuff, 1969, 1983a, 1983b, 1984). In this context, the Industrial Age required controlling responses. Basically, the person in the superior position directed the discriminations of the stimulus experience and controlled the subordinates' responses in the **S** ⟶ **R** conditioning paradigm. Thus, the teachers directed and controlled the students' memorization of facts and concepts of the implementation of conditioned operations responses. Likewise, supervisors directed and controlled the workers' performance of tasks.

Facilitative interpersonal processing characterizes the needs of the Electronics Age. Basically, superiors facilitated the participation of their subordinates in processing. Thus, teachers and managers alike responded to facilitate experiential exploring, personalized the resultant understanding of goals, and initiated and individualized action programs to achieve the goals. In so doing, they received their subordinates' images of the tasks to be performed or the problems to be solved.

Now, in the Information Age, totally new ways of processing interpersonally are called for. Again, with individuals processing entire data bases, methods must be developed to facilitate the interdependent sharing of the products of individual processing. Individuals need to get the images of others before sharing their own images and then negotiating merged images of the tasks or problems. In this manner, the processor maximizes the benefits from both individual and interpersonal processing.

To sum, just as with individual processing, the different ages require different methods of interpersonal processing which facilitate the individual processing. In particular, the Information Age requires the sharing and merging of individually processed responses, thus maximizing the contributions of both individual and interpersonal processing.

Individual Processing

The key to interdependent processing remains individual processing. Each individual engaged in interpersonal processing must process individually. Indeed, the interpersonal processing is only productive to the degree the individual processing was productive. If the individual processing of

77

the individual parties involved is not productive, then the interpersonal processing involves the sharing of meaningless responses.

We see in Figure 6-1 that each individual processes individually before processing interpersonally. Thus, we see how the individuals explore, understand and act upon values, content, personal and interpersonal information. It is only after they have processed individually that they share by getting and giving images of their responses.

In general, individual processing serves to transform the raw data of human experience into productive information, potentially usable for human purposes. This productive information may translate into different forms at different levels of processing. Thus, people may share and process interpersonally their images of missions or goals to be accomplished, objectives to be achieved, programs to be implemented, or tasks or steps to be acted upon.

For example, people may process their values individually in order to develop living, learning or working missions or goals. They may share their images with each other, as parents do in guiding their families, or teachers in directing their students, or employers in directing their employees. They share with the expectation that they will be able to negotiate a merged image of policy to guide their efforts as well as those for whom they are responsible.

In a similar manner, people may process content and personal and intrapersonal implications before sharing interpersonally the products of their individual processing efforts. Children, students and employees as well as parents, teachers and employers may share their definitions of operational objectives, programs, or action tasks or steps. Again, they process interpersonally in anticipation of merging their definitions.

Sometimes people may process simultaneously and interactively *all* the information and personal dimensions. In doing so, they may produce all of the levels of definitions of their responses: policy, goals, objectives, programs, tasks, steps. They elicit and then submit these definitions for

78

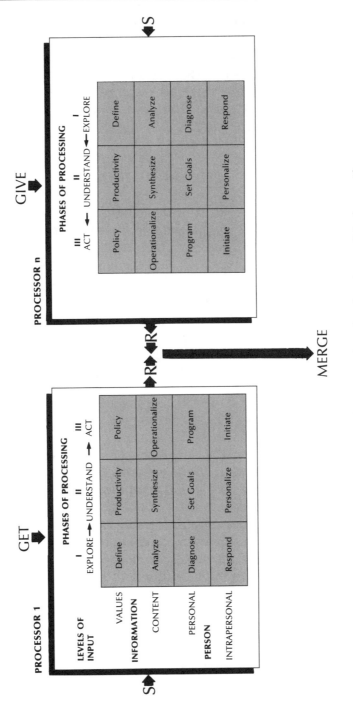

Figure 6-1. Interpersonal Processing in the Age of Information

negotiation in the interdependent operations of $S \longrightarrow P \longrightarrow R$ processing.

To sum, individual processing prepares the processors for interpersonal processing. The more productive the individual processing, the more productive are the uses of the products of the processing. These information products constitute the basis for interpersonal processing.

Interpersonal Processing

The purpose of individual processing is to produce productive information. The purpose of interpersonal processing is to produce still more productive information. Interpersonal processing emphasizes the interdependent processing of two or more people for purposes of producing productive information.

The means by which interpersonal processing is accomplished is sharing. People share their images of the goals to be achieved or the tasks to be performed. People work together to negotiate merged images of the goals or tasks.

The basis for interpersonal processing is empathic understanding. Empathy is the ability to enter another person's frame of reference and see the world through his or her eyes. The interpersonal skills which accomplish empathic understanding are the responding skills. Responding skills enable us to discriminate and communicate the other person's perceptions.

Basically, all interpersonal processing operates on the principle of reciprocal relations: people tend to relate to us the way we relate to them. Responding or being empathic to others elicits an attempt by others to be empathic with us. Thus, all parties are attempting to see the world through each others' eyes.

Moreover, if the individuals have maximized their individual processing and their interpersonal sharing, the likelihood is that the discrepancy in images will be minimal.

Indeed, when there is a large discrepancy, it will probably be for valid reasons such as the fact that one or more parties had failed to take some dimensions into consideration.

The merger of images is accomplished by problem-solving or decision-making processes. What we are trying to accomplish in merging images is a product or response that incorporates the best features and eliminates the vulnerabilities of all positions. Again, the greater the individual processing, the more facilitative will be the negotiations for merged responses.

We can see the critical nature of interpersonal processing in all areas of living, learning and working: in the development of ethics that will guide people through their lives; in the learning overview which compares teacher and learner images of skill applications, thus making learning instrumental for the learners' purposes; in the work assignment or performance review which enables both employer and employee to converge upon the same wavelength. Without interpersonal processing skills, life is a series of crises, where each diverged image leads to further distance and each apparent solution precipitates the next crisis.

Get, Give, Merge And Go

The outputs of individual processing, then, become the inputs of interpersonal processing. The individual processors produce their images of the policy, goals, objectives, programs, tasks, steps. They share these images with each other and process new images of products or responses.

In the "Get, Give, Merge and Go" program, the processors process interpersonally by "getting" and "giving" their images of the products to be produced or the responses to be performed. Depending upon expertise or authority, a lead person may "get" or elicit other people's images. The lead person may or may not facilitate the individual processing that produces those images.

If the lead person facilitates the processing of the subject matter, he or she may use the following interpersonal skills: *attending* personally to involve the other parties in processing; *responding* to their experience to facilitate their exploring; *personalizing* their goals in order to facilitate their understanding; *initiating* programs in order *to facilitate* their acting to produce a response. If the expert or authority does not facilitate the individual processing of others, he or she may simply respond *accurately* to elicit and personalize the others' images of the products or responses.

The products or responses of individual processing should be defined in functional terms so that all parties involved can process the various images. The products should present missions in specific terms; goals in measurable terms; objectives in operational terms; programs in planning terms; tasks in observable terms; steps in behavioral terms. Both in "getting" and "giving," the emphasis should be upon the functional terms of the products or responses.

Again, the process of negotiating merged images is primarily a process of problem solving or decision making. Basically, there are three options when sharing images: doing things "my way," "your way" or "our way." In negotiating a merged or converged image, we utilize both individual and organizational values as well as requirements to evaluate the alternative images. Those images which best satisfy both values and/or requirements are the merged or preferred image.

The processors then proceed to planning to act upon the merged image of the goal. This planning may also be accomplished interpersonally or it may be conducted by the individuals responsible for acting to achieve the goal.

To sum, the "Get, Give, Merge and Go" interpersonal processing program is enabled by individual processing. It is implemented by sharing and then merging images which the responsible parties go on to act upon. "Get, Give, Merge and Go" serves as a model for interpersonal processing in the Age of Information.

Interpersonal Processing Products

The product of interpersonal processing, then, is productive information. Productive information is information that is defined in operational terms for purposes of processing. Thus, the processors may compare or contrast, generalize or discriminate, classify or categorize the similarities and differences in the dimensions. For example, the processors may process their mission or goals interpersonally with mission statements as follows:

> To accomplish *(goals)*
> For *(populations)*
> By *(strategies)*

In a similar manner, the processors may process their objectives interpersonally with operational definitions as follows:

> *Who* or *what* is involved?
> *What* are they doing?
> *Why* and *how* are they doing it?
> *Where* and *when* are they doing it?
> *How well* are they doing it?

Likewise, the processors may process their programs interpersonally with plans or programs as follows:

> *Objectives*
> *Tasks*
> *Steps*
> *Milestones*
> *Timelines*

Finally, the processors may process their implementation programs interpersonally as follows:

> *Review*
> *Rehearse*
> *Revise*
> *Realize*
> *Recycle*

To sum, the products of individual processing are definitions of responses to be performed. These definitions are shared and processed interpersonally.

It is helpful to think of interpersonal processing as an obstetric team preparing to deliver a baby. The response is the baby. To the best of their ability, the team must be committed to birthing a perfect and healthy baby. This commitment to perfection must be reflected in the overriding values of the processors for productive responses.

The personal and institutional implications are clear. Not only do we teach and reinforce individual processing skills in our homes, schools and businesses but also interpersonal processing skills which add significant value to the products of our individual processing. Thus, participants in interpersonal processing share their images of the operationally defined objectives of their individual processing, negotiate new and more productive images, and prepare to act upon these merged images. This constant recycling of individual and interpersonal processing yields higher and higher levels of productivity.

In summary, the power of interpersonal processing lies in all parties to the processing: first, in their individual processing which enables them to produce productive definitions of responses; then in their interpersonal processing which adds value to their individual definitions. When all parties to a relationship have processed individually, then the product of interpersonal processing may be elevated exponentially. When all parties to a relationship have *not* processed individually, then the product of interpersonal processing will be decremental. Productive interpersonal processing enables productive individual processors to proactively preclude crises in their lives, their learning, and their work.

7.
Organizational Processing in the Age of Information

Human Technology, Inc., was not unlike most hierarchical organizations. Until seven years ago, I was not only the policymaker but also the operational leader. With one to two new projects each month, I was able to design each model the required systems were derived from and developed by the personnel. With the press of a new project each day, it became apparent that we could no longer operate in this manner. Accordingly, we attempted to increase organizational processing in four basic ways. At input, we attempted to increase the quantity and quality of information relevant to our activities. In processing, we decentralized both authority and responsibility for processing to personnel at the point of information flow. At output, we dedicated our processing to consumer productivity: our business was to keep our consumers in business! In feed-backing, we developed constant feedback on performance and productivity information for purposes of self-management. The results were astounding! Over the past seven years, the organization has grown more than 100% per year. Improved organizational processing leads to improved organizational productivity.

The different ages also require different organizational processing strategies. Thus, the Industrial Age emphasized mechanical processing. Basically, raw material inputs were transformed by machinery into finished products. Labor,

seen as an extension of the machine, operated by the principle of "working harder" and functioned only where it had
not yet been replaced by machinery. Feedback emphasized
results outputs since an infinite supply of resource inputs
was assumed. Supervision emphasized monitoring the entire delivery process.

During the Electronics Age, computer processing asserted
itself. Human and information resource inputs displaced
capital resource expenditures as the critical resource inputs
(Carkhuff, 1984; Carkhuff and Cannon, 1986; Carnavale, 1983).
Advancements in knowledge and the quality of labor converged upon the principle of "working smarter" in the workplace. Services complemented products as outputs. Productivity feedback emphasized resource efficiency as well as
results effectiveness. Participative management procedures
complemented supervisory monitoring of outputs as employees shared in determining courses of action to achieve goals.

Finally, organizational processing in the Information Age
requires human processing. The critical inputs are human
and information resources. Based upon the principle of
"thinking better" or more productively, the critical processes
emphasize the interaction of human and information resource
development. In turn, consumer benefits are added to product and service outputs. Feedback emphasizing both consumer and producer productivity is used largely for purposes
of self-management as supervisory controls are eliminated.

In conclusion, just as with individual and interpersonal
processing, the different ages require different methods of
organizational processing. In particular, the Information Age
requires human processing complemented by computer
and mechanical processing, thus maximizing the contributions of processing to organizational productivity.

Organizational Processing Operations

Organizational processing in the Age of Information emphasizes the contributions of human and information

resource variables. Not only are these variables the dominant resource inputs; they are also the prepotent source of processing.

We may view the operations of organizational processing in Figure 7-1. As may be seen, human resources (HR) and information resources (IR) dominate the capital resources ($R) that have traditionally accounted for resource inputs. In turn, the critical operations with the processing itself emphasize the synergistic interaction between human and information resource development (HRD ⟷ IRD): as personnel become more skilled, they contribute to advancements in knowledge; as advancements in knowledge are disseminated, personnel become more skilled. Together, these variables account for "thinking more" and "working less."

In addition to product and service, consumer benefits are incorporated as outputs. In so doing, we are guided by the principle of consumer productivity: the purposes of organization processing are to facilitate the productivity of our consumers, i.e., to help minimize the resource expenditures and maximize the results benefits of our customers. In effect, our business is to keep our customers in business.

Finally, feedback reflects several levels of productivity information: producer response performance; consumer productivity; producer productivity. Again, these indices of productivity are employed for purposes of improving individual performance at the delivery level and improvement of productivity at the unit and organizational levels.

Resource Inputs

We may take a more in-depth look at the operations of these critical variables. The data from economists' projections indicate that human and information resources in the form of skilled personnel inputs account for approximately 30–40% of economic growth in the Age of Information (Carkhuff, 1984; Carnavale, 1983). Capital resource expenditures which enable equipment and materials purchases

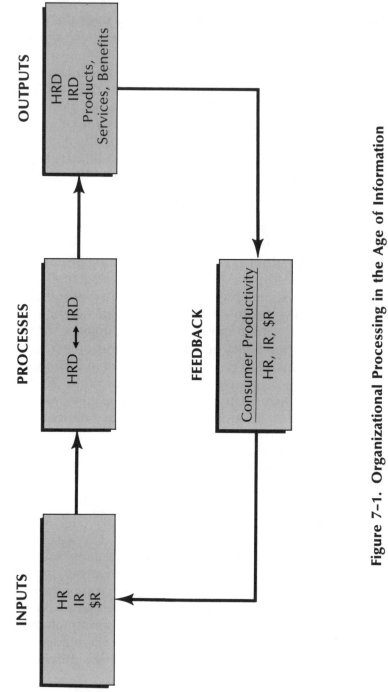

Figure 7–1. Organizational Processing in the Age of Information

account for approximately 15–20% of the variance. The implication is straightforward: the critical resource inputs are human and information resources. Capital, once dominant, is now a critical catalyst for organizational productivity.

Organizational Processing

According to the economists, human and information resource variables, alone and in interaction with each other, account for 50% of economic growth in the Age of Information (Carkhuff, 1984; Carnavale, 1983). In order to understand this organizational processing further, we must look at/analyze a typical organization (see Figure 7-2). As can be seen, the resource, production, marketing and distributing components interact with management, supervision and delivery functions. Within each of these cells created by the interactions, the processes take place: inputs, processing, outputs, feedbacking. These processes are constant within and between every component and function.

These processes incorporate both individual and interpersonal processing (see Figure 7-3). As can be seen, individuals process (P) stimulus (S) material individually, then share their responses (R) interpersonally and negotiate merged images of the responses. The new responses become stimulus inputs at the next level. Depending upon the size of the organization, the process may be replicated many times each day.

Basically, this means that *all personnel*, executive as well as delivery, *must be equipped with individual and interpersonal processing skills*. Clearly, these processing skills must be relevant to specific as well as complementary roles. Thus, policymakers, after processing both external information inputs and internal productivity feedback, develop the mission. Then the managers derive the goals from the mission and plan the operations for achieving the goals. Next, the supervisors derive the objectives from the management plan and develop the resources to achieve the objectives.

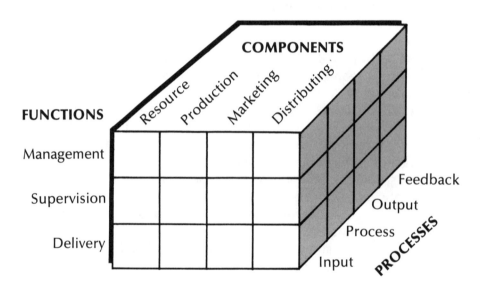

Figure 7–2. Components, Functions and Processes of Organizations

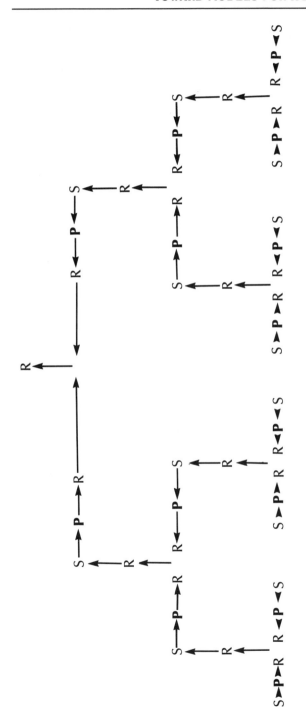

Figure 7-3. An Illustration of Individual and Interpersonal Processing Within Organizational Processing

Finally, the delivery personnel derive and perform the tasks involved. Thus, the responses at each level become stimulus inputs for processing at the next level.

Just as the process is constantly cycled to produce products and services, so is it constantly recycled to improve performance and productivity. Delivery task performance is assessed in achievement of the objectives, the objectives in achievement of the goals, the goals in the accomplishment of the mission. Again, the responses at each level become stimulus input for processing at the next level.

In a productive organization, this process occurs constantly at every level of function within every component. The personnel process individually and interpersonally for purposes of improving performance at their individual stations and productivity for their units and, finally, the organization. To sum, the responses within and between each level of each component become stimulus inputs for further productive processing.

Results Outputs

The critical addition to outputs in the Age of Information is consumer benefits. Consumer benefits are not simply indices of consumer satisfaction. Consumer benefits are defined by indices of consumer productivity:

$$\textbf{Consumer Productivity} \quad = \quad \frac{\textbf{Results Outputs}}{\textbf{Resource Inputs}}$$

This means that we should have tangible evidence of simultaneously increasing results outputs while decreasing resource inputs. Consumers will simply purchase what helps them to accomplish their own privatized goals most productively. Organizations that are not attuned to this ethic will themselves become unproductive, unprofitable and unknown.

Other critical outputs are added in the Age of Information. Since human and information resources are the most critical variables in both inputs and outputs, so do they become critical by-products in outputs. With high levels of inputs and processing, high levels of human and information resource development outputs will be produced. The highly developed personnel become valuable assets for internal and external uses. The highly developed information becomes valuable commodities for internal and external dissemination.

Information Feedback

Finally, feedback assesses and feeds back or returns information on not only individual response performance but also consumer and producer productivity. Response performance is assessed by the implementation of the operations needed to perform the task or achieve the objective. Consumer productivity is assessed by comparing the consumers' resource efficiency with the consumers' results effectiveness. Producer productivity is calculated by comparing the producer's resource efficiency with the accomplishment of the consumers' productivity:

$$\textbf{Producer Productivity} \quad = \quad \frac{\textbf{Consumer} \dfrac{\textbf{Results Outputs}}{\textbf{Resource Inputs}}}{\textbf{Producer} \quad \textbf{Resource Inputs}}$$

Over time and with iterations, the producer will attempt to increase effectiveness in terms of consumer productivity while increasing efficiency in resource investments. Again, these assessments are constantly fed back for purposes of improving individual performance and organizational productivity.

Improving Organizational Productivity

There are several strategies for improving organizational processing and, as a result, organizational productivity. Clearly, the first of these strategies has to do with improving the caliber or quality of both human and information resource inputs. Personnel who are productive processors will process information productively. Information which is inclusive and accurate will be inversely related to all other capital expenditures: *the better the information, the less the investment in other resources.*

In turn, the synergistic interaction of human and information resources defines productive organizational processing: *as human resources are developed, they contribute to the development of information resources and vice versa.*

The critical new ingredient in outputs is the focus upon consumer productivity. Again, consumer productivity will become the driving ethic of the Information Age. Simply stated, *those who make consumers productive will survive.*

Finally, feedback in the Age of Information emphasizes improving individual performance and organizational productivity. Producer productivity is defined by *reducing resource investments after meeting consumer requirements.*

All major improvements are contingent upon driving down both the responsibility and authority for processing to the people at the point of information flow. This means a dramatic reorganization of lines of authority. The delivery personnel become the critical processors in any organization. This means the learners or trainees in the classroom as well as the production or sales or service personnel in industry. Unless they process productively and immediately, raw data will not be transformed into productive information. Moreover, critical data will age, be distorted or lost to strategic processing personnel. Succinctly, children, learners and workers as well as parents, teachers and managers must learn to manage themselves and conduct their own processing in the Age of Information.

In summary, organizational processing in the Age of Information emphasizes human processing, complemented by other forms of processing. Human processing alone offers the prospect of potentially infinite productivity. By maximizing information inputs, we may minimize all other resource inputs. By maximizing human processing, we may maximize our results outputs.

The personal and institutional implications are clear:

1. Minimize other resource expenditures by maximizing information resource inputs.
2. Maximize human processing by teaching people to think productively, both individually and interpersonally, as well as organizationally.
3. Maximize human processing by decentralizing both responsibility and authority for thinking.
4. Maximize human productivity by facilitating dedication to the consumer productivity ethic.
5. Maximize individual performance improvement and organizational productivity by maximizing productivity feedback as input to processing.

These maxims are integrated in productive organizations which are held together by shared ethics or missions and dedicated to decentralized processing. By acting upon these maxims, we can look forward to individual processing that transforms raw data into productive information. In turn, interpersonal processing may add value to that productive information. Finally, the individual and interpersonal processing may take place in the context of organizational processing, where each individual knows how to process the products and services of his or her role to maximize the performance of others and the productivity of the organization.

In conclusion, the prospect of infinite human productivity is on the horizon in the Age of Information. It depends upon infinite information inputs. Above all, it depends upon infinite individual, interpersonal and organizational processing.

IV.
R & D in Human
Processing

8.
Individual Processing and Individual Performance

Dr. Bernard Berenson at American International College emphasizes human productivity in teaching his HRD graduate students, who are comprised of business, government and human service personnel, to **learn-to-learn** *before they do anything else. The students learn how to use their textbooks to develop their own skill programs. They learn how to analyze the components of knowledge available on each page; they analyze the facts. Synthesizing both concepts and facts, they build principles—at least one per page.*

This is a remarkable accomplishment since most books are written around a few facts and concepts and perhaps no more than one principle. For many authors, indeed, each new book constitutes little more than a variation on some original principle. Yet here are learners who are able to develop at least one principle per page.

More important, the students learn how to operationalize skills objectives from the principles. Then they go on to technologize the skill steps to achieve the skill objectives.

Again, with the exception of a few books—mostly math, vocational and technical texts—very few books are ever written about skills. That is interesting in itself because skills are the only things we can use. We cannot use knowledge if we cannot translate it into a skill and apply it. The power reflected in the students' **learning-to-learn** *skills is a quantum leap beyond any author's power. The students' power for improving their own personal performance is overwhelming.*

A number of studies of the effects of individual processing skills have been conducted, many of them by graduates of Berenson's programs (see Table 8-1). In every instance, the subjects were trained in both individual and interpersonal processing skills. A sample of studies emphasizing indices of living, learning and working yielded results that were positive and significant.

Living and Learning Performance

In 1970, the first training programs in individual and interpersonal processing skills was piloted at a home for delinquent youth (Carkhuff, Devine, Berenson and Griffin, 1974). The results indicated significant improvement on indices of physical, emotional and intellectual functioning, including one and one-half grade levels improvement over a year. In addition, there was a reduction in runaways from 25% to 12% of the youth. Most important, there was a reduction in recidivism of 34%. Finally, there was a reduction in crime of 34% in the communities from which the youth were drawn.

Hall (1978a, 1978b) replicated the institutional findings. Working at two different institutions for youth, he established significant growth in physical, emotional and intellectual indices. After initially finding only 6.2 to 6.0 months' intellectual improvement over a six-month period at the first institution, Hall demonstrated a 2.7 years' growth in intellectual achievement over a six-month period at the second institution with an improved version of training. In addition, he reduced recidivism at one institution from 50% to 28% and at a second from 26% to 12%. In turn, Steinberg and his associates replicated the results with institutionalized adult offenders, improving intellectual functioning more than one grade level in reading and more than three grade levels in math over a three-month period. In addition to significant physical and emotional changes, they reduced recidivism from 80% to 31%.

TABLE 8-1
INDIVIDUAL PERFORMANCE OUTCOMES

STUDY				METHOD		RESULTS		
ORGANIZATION	AUTHORS	DATE	POPULATION	MEASURES	TIME	TREATMENT	CONTROL	DIFF.
1. Training School, R.I.	Carkhuff, Devine, Berenson & Griffin	1974	120 youth	Physical	1 year	69%	46%	*
				Emotional	1 year	2.8	1.4	*
				Intellectual	1 year	7.6 Gr.	6.1 Gr.	*
				Runaways	1 year	12%	28%	*
2. Training School, N.Dak.	Hall	1978a	25 youth	Physical	1 year	3.8	2.7	*
				Emotional	1 year	3.1	2.1	*
				Intellectual	6 mos.	+6.2 mos.	+6.0 mos.	NS
				Recidivism	1 year	28%	50%	*
3. Training School, N.Dak.	Hall	1978b	55 youth	Physical	6 mos.	2.5	46%	*
				Emotional	6 mos.	3.0	1.4	*
				Intellectual	6 mos.	+2.6 Yr.	+6.0 mos.	*
4. Kalamazoo Jail, Mich.	Steinberg, Bellingham & Devine	1981	50 youth	Recidivism	1 year	12%	26%	*
5. Pontiac Schools, Mich.	Danley, Ahearne & Battenschlag	1975	270 youth (Learning Deficit)	Math Homework	6 mos.	+66%		*
				Reading " "	6 mos.	+37%		*
				School " "	6 mos.	+23%		*
				School Talk	6 mos.	+55%		*
				Parent Visits	6 mos.	+52%		*

101

TABLE 8-1 (Continued)

STUDY				METHOD		RESULTS		
ORGANIZATION	AUTHORS	DATE	POPULATION	MEASURES	TIME	TREATMENT	CONTROL	DIFF.
6. Children's Home, Mich.	Devine, Bellingham, Essex & Steinberg	1977	10 youth	Parent-Initiated Visits	6 mos.	+48%		*
				Discipline Problems	6 mos.	-31%		*
				Physical	6 mos.	3.0-3.8	2.3-3.1	*
				Behavior Self- & Other Care	6 mos.	2.7-3.1	1.7-3.4	*
				Responsiblity	6 mos.	1.7-2.9	1.4-3.0	*
				Interpersonal	6 mos.	1.3-2.9	2.1-3.2	*
				Runaway Intellectual	6 mos.	3.0	23.0	*
				Reading	6 mos.	7.9	6.7	*
				Spelling	6 mos.	5.5	5.0	*
				Math	6 mos.	5.0	4.5	*
7. Dallas Youth Diversion, Tex.	Collingwood, Douds, Williams & Wilson	1978	887 youth	Physical	2.5 yrs.	3.0	2.5	*
				Emotional	2.5 yrs	2.7	1.5	*
				Intellectual (Learn) Intellectual (Study)	2.5 yrs	2.6	1.5	*
			1,353 youth	Recidivism	2.5 yrs. 2.5 yrs.	2.9 10.7%	2.0 45.5%	* *

TABLE 8-1 (Continued)

STUDY				METHOD			RESULTS		
ORGANIZATION	AUTHORS	DATE	POPULATION	MEASURES	TIME	TREATMENT	CONTROL	DIFF.	
8. Springfield Urban League, Mass.	Berenson, Berenson, Berenson, Carkhuff, Griffin & Ransom		152 youth	Physical	3 mos.	4.61	3.89	*	
				Emotional	3 mos.	3.66	2.67	*	
				Intellectual	3 mos.	7.47 Gr.	6.08 Gr.	*	
				School Return	3 mos.	95%		*	
9. Equal Educa- tion Oppor- tunities Program, D.C.	Banks, Cannon, et. al.	1983	100 gov't employees	Work Quantity	1 year	+7%		*	
				Work Quality	1 year	+9%		*	
				Process Movement	1 year	+2.75 levels		*	
				IPS Skill Acquisition	1 year	+1.3 levels		*	
				IPS Skill Appl. Work Plans	1 year	89% positive		*	
				Task Ident. Reporting	1 year	74% positive		*	
				Procedures Information	1 year	77% positive		*	
				Appliance	1 year	75% positive		*	

TABLE 8-1 (Continued)

| STUDY | | | POPULATION | METHOD | | RESULTS | | |
ORGANIZATION	AUTHORS	DATE		MEASURES	TIME	TREATMENT	CONTROL	DIFF.
9. Equal Education Opportunities Program, DC				Individual Task Measures				
				Work Plan Usage (Weekly)	1 year	69%		*
				Work Plan Usage (Mo.)	1 year	90%		*
				Work Plan Value		82%		*
				Reporting Procedures (Mo.)	1 year	95%		*
				Reporting Procedure Value	1 year	85%		*
				Agency Task Measures				
				Role Clar.	1 year	60%		*
				Work Coor.	1 year	65%		*
				Work Planning	1 year	90%		*
				Work Producing	1 year	70%		*
				Crisis Reduction	1 year	40%		*
				Communication Improvement	1 year	70%		*
				Assignment Clarification	1 year	75%		*

TABLE 8-1 (Continued)

STUDY			METHOD			RESULTS		
ORGANIZATION	AUTHORS	DATE	POPULATION	MEASURES	TIME	TREATMENT	CONTROL	DIFF.
10. Department of Education, D.C.	Pierce	1983	100 Employees	Recognize Diff.	6 mos.	3.83	2.67	*
				Reflecting	6 mos.	3.62	2.20	*
				Sharing Percep.	6 mos.	3.59	2.36	*
				Resolve Diff.	6 mos.	3.44	2.44	*
				Recognize Bias	6 mos.	4.00	2.38	*
				Recognize Disc.	6 mos.	3.95	2.60	*
				Recognize Fairness	6 mos.	3.50	2.33	*
				Plan Time	6 mos.	3.67	2.17	*
				Plan Goals	6 mos.	4.07	2.52	*
				Plan Action	6 mos.	3.92	2.52	*
				Monitor Work	6 mos.	4.06	2.60	*
				Analyze Staff	6 mos.	3.50	2.17	*
				Make Assign.	6 mos.	3.85	2.49	*
				Prepare Meeting	6 mos.	3.67	2.33	*
				Conduct Discussion	6 mos.	3.74	2.56	*
				Set Expectation	6 mos.	3.59	2.43	*
				Monitor Perf.	6 mos.	3.73	2.28	*
				Motivate Perf.	6 mos.	3.75	2.62	*
				Time Savings	6 mos.	13,900 hrs.		NA
				$ Savings	6 mos.	$128,897		NA
				R.O.I.	6 mos.	3.24		NA

TABLE 8-1 (Continued)

STUDY			METHOD			RESULTS		
ORGANIZATION	AUTHORS	DATE	POPULATION	MEASURES	TIME	TREATMENT	CONTROL	DIFF.
11. Human Technology, Va.	Carkhuff	1983	13 Business Employees	$ Output Personnel Input Ind. Perf. Profit	1 year 1 year 1 year 1 year	+25% −16% +48% +50%		* * * *
12. New Careers, Mass.	Carkhuff	1983	100 Unemployed	Employment	2 years 13 yrs	88% 80%		NA NA

*—Significant differences between treatment and control groups

NS—Non-significant differences

NA—Not applicable

Other investigators sought to replicate these findings in non-institutional settings. Working with learning deficit youth, Danley and her associates (Danley, Ahearn and Battenschlag, 1975) established significant improvement in completion of homework assignments, school talk at home, parent visits to school and youth discipline problems. In turn, Devine and his associates (Devine, Bellingham, Essex and Steinberg, 1977) established significant improvement in behavioral as well as intellectual indices. In the process, they reduced runaways from a mean of 23 per individual to a mean of three per youth. Collingwood and his associates also demonstrated significant improvement on physical, emotional and intellectual indices, with intellectual achievement improving 2.7 years over a six-month period. They also reduced delinquincy recidivism over 2.5 years from a base rate of over 45% to just over 10%.

The most refined learning skills program was conducted by Berenson and his associates (Berenson, Berenson, Berenson, Carkhuff, Griffin and Ransom, 1978). The primary goal of the program was to teach school "dropouts" learning-to-learn basic communication and computation skills. The learning-to-learn skills emphasized individual processing skills: exploring or analyzing content, understanding or synthesizing content, acting or operationalizing content. The learning skills were applied directly to learning the following content areas: learning-to-learn reading; learning-to-learn mathematics. Learner functioning in reading and math improved more than one grade with an investment of 13 hours of teaching time over a three-month period. Moreover, 95% of the students returned to school.

Working Performance

In working applications, a number of demonstrations were conducted and assessed. Banks and his associates (Banks, Cannon, Carkhuff, Friel, McCune and Pierce, 1983) trained employees in an information agency in individual and interpersonal processing skills. The productivity goals focused upon implementing regulations, processing grants, and providing technical assistance to the states. The objectives emphasized using a management system, work plans, reporting procedures, and communication skills to achieve the productivity goals. The training program emphasized individual processing and problem solving skills in conjunction with interpersonal processing skills. All 100 personnel—from clerks to the assistant secretary—were trained in the processing skills in relation to their roles in developing their work plans and implementing the management design. Every phase of process and outcome was assessed. The employees demonstrated significantly positive movement on the following indices: process movement, acquisition, application, task performance, agency objectives. Moreover, the employees demonstrated significant improvement in measures of productivity: improving overall work quantity seven percent and overall work quality nine percent.

Pierce (1983) also applied individual and interpersonal processing skills to the workplace. Working with decision makers, he established productivity goals emphasizing cost avoidance savings. Analyzing the contextual task requirements, Pierce designed an individual and interpersonal skills-based, supervisory training program emphasizing traditional planning and monitoring supervisory skills. Pierce was able to establish significant improvement on a variety of planning and implementing indices. Most important, he demonstrated savings of nearly 14,000 hours and over $100,000 over a six-month period. It is noteworthy that the supervisory personnel were almost unanimous in their endorsement of the processing skills as the prepotent sources of effect in supervision.

In another working application, the staff was assessed in terms of its individual and organizational processing and trained in the areas of its vulnerabilities (Carkhuff, 1983). First, the staff was assessed in relation to its ability to plan, process and assess within their policy-making, management, supervisory and delivery role functions. Second, the staff was assessed in relation to its individual physical, emotional and intellectual functioning. The organizational function assessments emphasized planning, processing and assessing deficits. The individual function assessments emphasized motivational, interpersonal, learning and teaching or communicating deficits. Process-based training in the deficit areas was offered and the processes and outcomes were assessed. The levels of process movement, acquisition, application and transfer of processing skills were high. Moreover, over a one-year period, individual output was improved by 48% while reducing resource input by 16% and improving individual profitability by 76%. In turn, organizational output was improved by 25% while reducing personnel resources by 16%. Most important, organizational profitability increased 50%.

Finally, a comprehensive community-based program was addressed to an entire Northeastern inner city (Carkhuff, 1983b). Community needs were assessed, and living, learning and working goals were established for both adults and youth. Contextual tasks were analyzed and instructional systems designed to accomplish the tasks. An individual and interpersonal processing-based curriculum was installed. The leading performers from each wave of trainees became the trainers of the next wave of trainees. While thousands of people were involved, samples of performance indicated the following: a reduction of home crises to 1.5 per month; a reduction of community crises to one per six months; improvement in youth grades of 1.4 levels; a reduction of school crises to one per month; 55% continuance of adults in college. Most critical, 80% of previously unemployed adults were productively employed 13 years later. The potential leverage of such processing-based programs is very impressive.

In summary, the research base of human processing is established. Clearly, human processing is a potent effect on all indices of living, learning and working. We may conclude that it is a necessary but not sufficient condition of all individual performance where changing data bases are involved. It may serve complementarily with other sources of learning such as social learning and conditioning. It may also serve synergistically with other sources of productivity improvement such as interpersonal and organizational processing.

9.
Interpersonal Processing and Unit Productivity

Ed Feder is an organizational development specialist with a large oil company (Feder, 1985). His efforts have been devoted to improving organizational productivity. His methods emphasize team-building and team problem-solving. The team-building and problem-solving programs are based upon interpersonal processing skills. Feder applied his efforts in seven different settings as part of his productivity improvement experiment.

The phases and stages of team problem-solving may be viewed in Figure 9-1. As can be seen, the phases emphasize getting the employee's (E's) image, giving the supervisor's (S's) image, negotiating a merged image, and going on to the next stage of problem analysis. In turn, the stages emphasize analyzing the problem, the reason for the problem, and the direction of the solution. Thus, the supervisor and employee get, give and merge images of the problems, then the reasons, and finally the directions which they go on to plan and implement. This interpersonal processing is called "Get, Give, Merge and Go."

An illustration of one of Feder's productivity improvement projects may be viewed in Table 9-1. As can be seen, Feder began by conducting a needs assessment and determining the intervention strategies. Next, he obtained support from management and other sources before embarking upon developing the program. The essence of the implementation involved sharing and priortizing problems and solutions with field leaders, then planning and implementing the projects. Finally, Feder evaluated the outcomes of the projects.

PHASES OF IPS

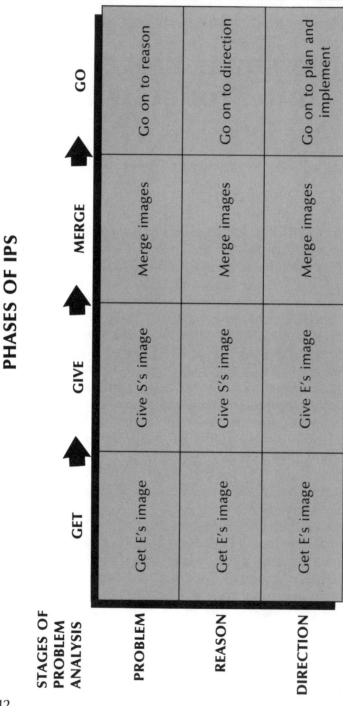

Figure 9–1. The Phases and Stages of Team Problem-Solving

TABLE 9-1

PRODUCTIVITY IMPROVEMENT PROGRAM PHASES				
I **Needs Assessment**	II **Intervention Strategy**	III **Program Preparation**	IV **Program Implementation**	V **Program Evaluation**
• Diagnosis • Analysis	• Training • Team Building • Problem Solving • Goal Setting • Measurement	• Management Support • Field Staff Support • Division Support	• Strategy • Program Development • Program Implementation	• Results • Costs • PIP Costs

Productivity Improvement

The results of Feder's productivity improvement programs may be viewed in Table 9-2. As can be seen, over a one-year period, in the seven projects which constituted the experiment, Feder and his associates were able to save more then $12,000,000 through improving daily production and cost avoidance. In turn, the cost of the improvements in productivity were calculated at less than one million dollars. The cost of the person/hour time to conduct the project may be viewed in Table 9-3. As may be noted, the cost of $17,313, together with the improvement costs, totaled just under one million dollars. Thus, the one-year return-on-investment was more than 12:1.

The most noteworthy conclusion is the extraordinary leverage of interpersonal processing skills-based intervention methodologies. With team-building and team problem-solving programs based upon IPS procedures, Feder and his associates were able to produce dramatic improvements in

TABLE 9-3

PRODUCTIVITY IMPROVEMENT PROGRAM COSTS		
ENGINEERS	$36.79/hour × 35 hours =	$ 1,287.65
FOREMEN	$24.14/hour × 54 hours =	1,303.56
SUPERINTENDANTS	$35.10/hour × 3 hours =	105.30
SENIOR FOREMEN	$25.75/hour × 3 hours =	77.25
ED	20 days =	5,000.00
	EXPENSES	$10,000.00
		$17,773.76

TABLE 9-2

ORGANIZATIONAL PRODUCTIVITY OUTCOMES

STUDY FOCUS	METHOD MEASURE	TIME	RESULTS SAVINGS	COST
1. Reduce Flowline Back Pressure	Daily Production (Barrels of Oil)	1 Year	$ 1,440,000	$100,000
2. Increase Staff to Impact Lost Revenue	Daily Production	1 Year	$ 270,000	$100,000
3. Reduce Well Back Pressure	Daily Production	1 Year	$ 3,348,000	$537,500
4. Reduce Well Back Pressure	Daily Production	1 Year	$ 6,480,000	$150,000
5. Get Vessel to Work	Daily Production	1 Year	$ 182,500	$ 3,000
6. Eliminating Environmental Problems	Cost Avoidance	1 Year	$ 1,200	$ 730
7. Repairing Gas Plant	Daily Production	1 Year	$ 800,000	$100,000
		1 Year TOTALS	$12,521,700	$991,230

productivity. Feder's work illustrates the potentially far-reaching effects of interpersonal processing skills upon organizational productivity in the Age of Information.

Interpersonal Productivity

More than 160 studies of the effects of interpersonal processing skills upon the individual performance of nearly 160,000 recipients in living, learning and working contexts have been summarized (Carkhuff, 1983b). Overall, the results were positive: 96% of the studies and 92% of the indices were positive and significant. The conclusion is inescapable: when interpersonal processing skills are introduced, there is only a random chance of failure in terms of significantly improving individual performance.

A sample of ten new studies focusing upon organizational productivity improvement in the working context demonstrates the efficacy of the interpersonal-skills-based "Get, Give, Merge and Go" (GGMG) interpersonal processing approaches (see Table 9-4). The first of these studies emphasized implementing an interpersonal-skills-based performance management system (PMS) in a Southwestern aerospace firm (Friel and Pierce, 1983). Other ingredients in the PMS included performance appraisal, work incentive and employee development systems related to the IPS system. Training more than six hundred managers and impacting 10,000 employees, the demonstrators were able to establish nearly $6,000,000 in cost avoidance savings over three years. With program costs of around $200,000, the return-on-investment (R.O.I.) was 29:1.

Working with a "low-technology, labor intensive" service company, Zigon (1983, 1984) designed and implemented an IPS-based PMS. Other ingredients in his system included Gilbert's (1978) trouble-shooting and job-modeling systems, Feeney's (1976) feedback technology, Tosti's (1981) reward techniques and Fournies' (1978) coaching skills. Training 1,000 managers responsible for 4,000 employees, the author

TABLE 9-4

ORGANIZATIONAL PRODUCTIVITY OUTCOMES

| ORGANIZATION | STUDY | | | METHOD | | RESULTS | | |
	AUTHORS	DATE	MANAGERS (Employees)	MEASURES	TIME	SAVINGS	COST	R.O.I.
1. General Dynamics, Tex.	Friel and Pierce	1983	645 (10,000)	Cost Avoidance	3 years	$5,996,250	$203,175	29:1
2. Yellow Freight, Kans.	Zigon	1984	1,000 (4,000)	Performance Improvement	13 mos.	$3,118,000	$500,000	6:1
3. Human Technology, Va.	Carkhuff and Cannon	1985	10 (30)	Performance Improvement	5 years	$2,500,000	$100,000	25:1
4. Electronics, Calif.	Shultz and Rowe	1984	240 (640)	Cost Avoidance	3 years	$2,128,507	$ 75,600	28:1
5. Hood Dairy Products, Mass.	McClain 1983	1982,	52 (520)	Performance Improvement	1 year	$1,186,800	$100,000	10:1

Table 9-4 (Continued)

ORGANIZATIONAL PRODUCTIVITY OUTCOMES

| ORGANIZATION | STUDY | | | METHOD | | | RESULTS | | |
	AUTHORS	DATE	MANAGERS (Employees)	MEASURES	TIME	SAVINGS	COST	R.O.I.
6. AMOCO, La.	Feder	1984	14 (656)	Performance Improvement	1 year	$496,000	$48,500	10:1
7. Abitibi-Price, Canada	Brillinger and Friel	1982	55 (750)	Performance Improvement	1 year	$300,000	$60,000	5:1
8. Convair, Calif.	Douds	1982	181 (2,000)	Cost Avoidance	6 mos.	$252,065	$50,000	5:1
9. General Dynamics, Calif.	Shultz	1982	250 (8,000)	Cost Avoidance	3 mos.	$250,000	$50,000	5:1
10. ARCO, Alaska	Holder	1983	28 (450)	Cost Avoidance	3 mos.	$161,462	$15,000	10:1

found that the firm could demonstrate more the $3,000,000 worth of performance improvement in 13 months. The R.O.I. of 6:1 is impacted by the extraordinary start-up costs of the entire human resource development (HRD) unit.

In turn, Carkhuff and Cannon (1986) implemented an IPS-based performance improvement program in a knowledge industry. They emphasized two basic ingredients: intensive in-service training to upgrade personnel in IPS and "state-of-the-art" technologies; and intensive interactions with customers in order to shape tailor-made products. The authors found gains of over $2,500,000 over a five-year period, posting 25:1 R.O.I. against an investment of approximately $20,000 per year.

Shultz and Rowe (1982, 1983), Douds (1982) and Holder (1984) all replicated the essential IPS-PMS interpersonal processing findings in manufacturing contexts. They found cost avoidance savings ranging from hundreds of thousands of dollars over a three- month period to more than $2,000,000 over a three-year period. Their R.O.I.'s ranged from 5:1 to 28:1.

McClain (1982, 1983) made two demonstrations of supervisory training. He demonstrated GGMG communications skills applications ranging from 80% to 93%. The performance improvement value ranged over $1,000,000 over a one-year period. The R.O.I. was 10:1. In turn, Feder (1984) conducted a series of IPS-based team problem-solving projects in the oil industry. In total, he demonstrated nearly $500,000 in performance improvement with a 10:1 R.O.I.

Brillinger and his associates (Brillinger and Friel, 1983) trained production and delivery supervisors in individual and interpersonal processing skills. Working in problem-solving teams, the personnel addressed all kinds of operational problems using the acronym PRIDE: problem identification, reason identification, inventing solutions, delivering solutions, evaluating results. They obtained $300,000 in performance improvement dollar savings and a 5:1 R.O.I. over a one-year period.

The effectiveness and efficiency of IPS-based management systems appears well documented in terms of organizational productivity improvement. With the exception of a few programs, most notably Zigon's with his extraordinary start-up costs, there appears to be a direct-line correlation between the dollar savings and the duration of the program: as time increases, savings increase.

One important defect in the GGMG programs is the lack of employee training. While managers are trained in individual and interpersonal processing skills, employees are not (Carkhuff, 1984). Real explosions in productivity improvement will not take place until line personnel are treated as critical sources of effect. Delivery personnel are, after all, most often the persons at the critical points of information flow (Carkhuff and Cannon, 1986). Productive interdependent processing involving all personnel is a requirement of the Information Age.

In summary, the IPS-based performance improvement programs have been highly productive in training managers and supervisors to intervene effectively and efficiently with their employees. In training programs involving more than 2,000 managers and nearly 25,000 employees, GGMG has demonstrated high levels of skill applications and bottom-line savings (Carkhuff, 1983a, 1983b, 1984). By processing interpersonally, the managers are able to negotiate more accurate definitions of the tasks to be performed. GGMG generates significant productivity improvements by preventing the cumulated crises that the authoritarian "Give and Go" style of supervision tends to elicit, crises that are compounded many times over by the unending flow of changing data in the Information Age.

In conclusion, it is clear that in the Age of Information, two conditions contribute to maximizing human productivity: the *individual processing* of the information and the *interpersonal processing* of the information. Together, these human processing skills maximize human productivity.

10.
Organizational Processing and Organizational Productivity

The fastest-growing companies in America made a dramatic public debut in *INC.* magazine in 1979, with repeat performances each year since. The original *INC. 100* described America's fastest-growing publicly held companies (Ketchum, 1984; Sammons, 1983) and their executives (Hartman, 1983). To this group was added in 1984 the *INC. 500*, the country's fastest-growing privately held companies (Hartman, 1984).

The significance of these *INC.* lists is found in their impact upon the American economy (see Table 10-1). For example, in 1979–1983, the 100 fastest-growing publicly held companies had a weighted average compounded annual growth rate of 115% and total sales growth of more than 2,000%. In turn, the 500 fastest-growing privately held companies had a weighted average compounded annual growth rate of 82%, and a total growth rate of nearly 1,000% over the 1979–1983 period. Consider that the *Fortune 500* firms were averaging about 4% per year growth or 17% compounded growth over the same four-year period. Clearly, the fastest-growing companies are critical sources of economic growth in these United States.

At the same time, in the employment area, the 100 fastest-growing publicly held companies have increased employment

TABLE 10-1

IMPACT OF FAST-GROWING COMPANIES UPON U.S. ECONOMY

	INC. 100	INC. 500	FORTUNE 500
Yearly Average Compounded Growth Rate	115%	82%	4%
Total Economic Growth (1979–1983)	2,030%	992%	17%
Total Employment Growth (1979–1983)	835%	402%	−11%

by over 50% during the last year and over 800% for the past five years. Similarly, the 500 fastest-growing privately held corporations have increased employment over 400% over the past five years, averaging 30% to 35% per year. Again, consider the fact that the "corporate giants" of the *Fortune 500* have lost more than 10% of their employees over this five-year period. Clearly, the fastest-growing companies are critical sources of employment opportunities in the United States.

Together, these fast-growing publicly and privately held firms possess the keys to the continuation of robust growth in the U.S. economy. It may be hypothesized that the leaders of these firms are responding to different cues and initiating with different intentions in this constantly changing

Age of Information. In the interest of pursuing these hypotheses, questions concerning the productive ingredients of these growth efforts were formulated and presented to the C.E.O.'s of these companies.

The questions emphasized the leaders' perceptions of the critical ingredients of their efforts. The questions revolved around their perceptions of the organizational components, functions and processes involved:

What are the critical organizational components?

What are the critical organizational functions?

What are the critical organizational processes?

In the interest of comparative data, sample groups of leaders from both the private and public sectors were also surveyed.

Surveying Sources of Productivity: Methods

The method employed was to survey the Chief Executive Officers (C.E.O.'s) of the *INC. 100* and *INC. 500* firms. The questionnaires employed open-ended questions before structured questions in order to obtain the unique views of the C.E.O.'s. The questionnaires were formulated by the author, based upon previous studies of sources of organizational productivity.

Corporate Characteristics

Twenty-four C.E.O.'s of *INC. 100* firms and 89 C.E.O.'s of *INC. 500* firms responded to the surveys. The total of 113 respondents constitutes a sample of nearly 20% of 600 of the fastest-growing public and private corporations. We may say this sample is representative of C.E.O.'s of fast-growing corporations who respond to productivity surveys.

Of the 24 *INC. 100* corporations, 71% are engaged in manufacturing, 25% in service industries, and 4% in mining. In turn, of the 89 *INC. 500* firms, 42% are engaged in manufacturing, 56% in service industries and 2% in mining.

The impact of the surveyed corporations upon the economy may be seen in Table 10-2. As can be seen, the publicly held corporations had a yearly average compounded growth rate of 92%, culminating in total economic growth of 1,257% for the 1979–1983 period. In turn, the privately held corporations had a yearly average compounded growth

TABLE 10-2

IMPACT OF SURVEYED COMPANIES
UPON U.S. ECONOMY

	INC. 100 (N = 24 Public Corporations)	INC. 500 (N = 89 Private Corporations)
Yearly Average Compounded Sales Growth Rate	92%	83%
Total Economic Growth (1979–1983)	1,257%	1,032%
Yearly Average Compounded Employment Growth Rate	58%	58%
Total Employment Growth (1979–1983)	530%	519%

rate of 83% and total economic growth of 1,032% for the same period. The 24 publicly held corporations have lower sales growth totals than the entire *INC. 100* totals while the 89 privately held corporations have growth totals slightly higher than the entire *INC. 500* totals.

In the employment area, the publicly held corporations' annual average compounded growth rate of 58% cumulates to a total employment growth of 530% for the 1979–1983 period. The privately held corporations' annual average compounded growth rate of 58% cumulates to 519% for the same period. The publicly held corporations' employment totals are lower than the entire *INC. 100* totals while the privately held corporations' totals are higher than the entire *INC. 500* totals.

As a whole, the sample of the fastest-growing public and private companies appeared representative of the overall data on the *INC. 100* and *INC. 500* corporations. It should be noted, however, that the comparison of the *INC. 100* with the *INC. 500* skews the data in favor of the 100. The averages of the publicly held firms appear to reflect more productivity than the privately held firms. In reality, the top 100 fastest-growing privately held firms from the *INC. 500* list compare very favorably with the *INC. 100*.

Questionnaires

The unstructured and structured questionnaires appear in Tables 10-3 and 10-4. As can be seen, the unstructured items—surveyed first—emphasize the C.E.O.'s personal experience of the ingredients critical to the organization's growth. The inquiries are open-ended and calculated to elicit the C.E.O.'s untutored or uninfluenced experience.

In all instances, the C.E.O.'s were asked to rate each ingredient from 1 (unimportant) to 10 (extremely important). In all instances, the opportunity was provided for the C.E.O.'s to add critical ingredients of their own creation. Interested readers may choose to take the survey, themselves,

TABLE 10-3

QUESTIONNAIRE: Ingredients of Exemplary Organizations

BACKGROUND INFORMATION

Your Name: _____ Your Company: _____

Describe Your Position: _____

Describe the major products and/or services provided by your company:

_____

_____

TELEPHONE INTERVIEW

Would you be willing to discuss your ideas about exemplary organizations in a brief telephone interview with Dr. John R. Cannon, Chief Executive Officer of Human Technology, Inc.? _____ Yes _____ No

If yes...

What is your phone number? ( ) _____—_____
                                    Area
                                    Code

What is the best time to reach you? _____ : __ AM. PM.

INGREDIENTS OF SUCCESS

Please list, in order of importance, the ingredients you believe are critical to your organization's exemplary performance. Please complete this list before proceeding to the next page.

TABLE 10-4

QUESTIONNAIRE: Ingredients of Exemplary Organizations

RATINGS

Listed below are potential ingredients of exemplary organizations. In each category, rate each ingredient using the following scale:

10 = Extremely Important

↑

1 = Unimportant

NOTE: You may use the same number more than once in any category.

Ratings   Ingredients

INPUTS
_____ CAPITAL RESOURCES (e.g., financing, high tech equipment)
_____ HUMAN RESOURCES (e.g., skilled personnel)
_____ INFORMATION RESOURCES (e.g., analyzed information)
_____ OTHER, PLEASE LIST: _____

PROCESSING
_____ COMPUTER PROCESSING (e.g., automated data processing)
_____ MECHANICAL PROCESSING (e.g., production by machinery)
_____ HUMAN PROCESSING (e.g., creative problem solving)
_____ OTHER, PLEASE LIST: _____

OUTPUTS
_____ PRODUCTS (e.g., most effective and cost-efficient)
_____ SERVICES (e.g., tailored to consumer needs)
_____ BENEFITS (e.g., demonstration of tangible results)
_____ OTHER, PLEASE LIST: _____

FEEDBACK
_____ MONITORING (e.g., micromanagement)
_____ FEEDBACK (e.g., recycling information)
_____ SELF-MANAGEMENT (e.g., personnel managing themselves)
_____ OTHER, PLEASE LIST: _____

ORGANIZATIONAL COMPONENTS
_____ RESOURCES (e.g., capital, labor)
_____ PRODUCTION (e.g., product production and services delivery)
_____ MARKETING (e.g., strategic and selling)
_____ DISTRIBUTION (e.g., fulfillment and servicing)
_____ OTHER, PLEASE LIST: _____

ORGANIZATIONAL FUNCTIONS
_____ POLICY (e.g., mission and strategic planning)
_____ MANAGEMENT (e.g., planning and implementing operations)
_____ SUPERVISION (e.g., monitoring and facilitating)
_____ DELIVERY (e.g., assembly and servicing)
_____ OTHER, PLEASE LIST: _____

at this time in order to compare their experiences with those of the C.E.O.'s of a sample of the fastest-growing companies.

Sources of Productivity: Results

The sources of productivity were indicated by both unstructured and structured survey questions. The unstructured questions yielded open-ended responses that were somewhat random and perhaps even benign. Yet these responses were consistent with the structured responses which were more revealing. The structured responses clarified the relative significance of the ingredients posited by respondents. In other words, the structured responses laid out "what really counts."

Open-Ended Responses

A sample of the open-ended responses elicited by the unstructured questions may be found in Table 10-5. As can be able seen, the respondents mentioned every category of organizational components, functions and processes.

The components mentioned included the following: R & D based upon corporate long-term vision; human resource development and deployment based upon corporate needs; marketing initiatives based upon consumer requirements; "state-of-the-art" production facilities and equipment; personalized distribution emphasizing customer service.

The organizational functions mentioned included the following: defined policies and priorities from visionary policy makers; management leadership in planning and interactive communication in implementing; active, "hands on" supervision; long-term, multi-talented employees.

The organizational processes included the following: dedicated personnel, innovative ideas and adequate capital as resource inputs; adaptable personnel who are eager to

128

TABLE 10-5

SAMPLE OF UNSTRUCTURED RESPONSES

ORGANIZATIONAL COMPONENTS
- Research and Development
- Human Resource Deployment
- Marketing Initiative
- "State-of-the-Art" Production Facilities
- Personalized Distribution

ORGANIZATIONAL FUNCTIONS
- Defined Policies and Priorities
- Management Leadership
- Management Communication
- Active, "Hands On" Supervision
- Long-Term, Multi-Talented Employees

ORGANIZATIONAL PROCESSES
  INPUTS
- Dedicated Personnel
- Innovative Ideas
- Adequate Capital

PROCESSING
- Adaptable and Trainable Personnel
- Control of Information Flow
- Mechanical Problem Prevention

OUTPUTS
- Quality Products
- Customer Service
- Guided by Consumer Requirements

FEEDBACKING
- Performance Feedback
- Consumer Feedback
- Consultant Feedback

be trained to think in corporate terms, control of information flow and mechanical problem prevention as processing ingredients; quality controlled products, customer responsive service and consumer responsive products and services as results outputs; performance, consumer and consultant feedback to improve productivity.

Structured Responses

A summary of the means or averages of the structured responses appears in Table 10-6. As can be seen, there is an extraordinary consistency across groups in the relative ratings of the most critical ingredients: the marketing component; the management function; human resource inputs; human processing; service outputs; feedbacking for self-management. It should be noted that the variability in ratings was more restrictive for the privately owned corporations. However, for our purposes, the important phenomenon is that the relative ratings of critical ingredients were consistent. Overall, the highest rated ingredient was human processing or creative problem solving. Human processing was clearly supported by human resource or skilled personnel inputs who were adaptable and trainable in processing skills. Thus, the two highest rated sources of productivity and the only dimensions averaging ratings over 9.0 on 10-point scales involved skilled humans capable of learning to think productively.

Within the organizational components, both the publicly and privately held corporations tended to rate the marketing related component of distribution higher than the other components. The publicly held corporations tended to rate the resource component higher than the privately held. In turn, the privately held corporations tended to rate the production component higher than their public counterparts.

Within the organizational functions, all other functions for both public and private corporations were modulated to support or implement the management planning functions.

130

TABLE 10-6

SUMMARY OF MEANS OF STRUCTURED RESPONSES		
	INC. 100 (N = 24 Public Corporations)	INC. 500 (N = 89 Private Corporations)
ORG. COMPONENTS		
RESOURCES	8.5	7.9
PRODUCTION	7.9	8.4
MARKETING	9.6*	8.7*
DISTRIBUTION	8.8	8.4
ORG. FUNCTIONS		
POLICY	8.0	7.5
MANAGEMENT	8.7*	8.6*
SUPERVISION	7.5	7.7
DELIVERY	7.3	7.7
ORG. PROCESSES		
INPUTS		
CAPITAL	6.4	7.0
HUMAN	9.0*	9.1*
INFORMATION	7.0	6.2
PROCESSING		
COMPUTER	6.0	6.3
MECHANICAL	4.6	5.2
HUMAN	9.4*	9.1*
OUTPUTS		
PRODUCTS	7.1	8.0
SERVICES	8.9*	9.2*
BENEFITS	8.7	8.0
FEEDBACKING		
MONITORING	7.0	7.1
RECYCLING	5.8	7.4
SELF-MANAGEMENT	9.0*	8.4*

*Top-rated dimension in category

This includes policy making as well as supervision and delivery functions.

Within the organizational process, both public and private corporations subordinated other resources to human resource inputs: public corporations rated information resources inputs slightly higher and private corporations rated capital resource inputs slightly higher. Both public and private corporations subordinated, in order, computer processing and non-intelligent mechanical processing to human processing. Public corporations rated consumer benefits higher and private corporations rated products higher while both converged upon customer services as outputs. Finally, public corporations rated monitoring higher and private corporations rated recycling higher while both emphasized self-management as the primary purpose of feedbacking.

Comparative Data

Preliminary comparative data may be found in Table 10-7. There a sample of executives of private sector corporations which, while of similar size, were not among the fastest-growing companies was surveyed. In addition, a sample of executives in public sector state and federal agencies was surveyed. As can be seen, the private executives' ratings were consistent with those of the INC. 100 and 500 executives. However, the public sector executives deviated on a number of items.

In addition, while the private sector control executives' averages were consistent with the ratings of the INC. executives, the ratings were in general depressed and the variability constricted. There were no real high ratings. Beyond hypothesizing conservatism, it is almost as if these executives knew what ingredients counted but were reluctant to "go out on a limb" to endorse those ingredients too formidably.

The public sector executive ratings were higher and more variable. They differed with the others on the significance

TABLE 10-7

	INC. 100 (N = 24 Public Corporations)	INC. 500 (N = 89 Private Corporations)
SUMMARY OF MEANS OF CONTROL RESPONSES		
ORG. COMPONENTS		
RESOURCES	8.0	9.0*
PRODUCTION	7.5	8.2
MARKETING	8.6*	8.2
DISTRIBUTION	8.3	7.5
ORG. FUNCTIONS		
POLICY	7.4	8.0
MANAGEMENT	7.9*	8.5*
SUPERVISION	7.1	7.9
DELIVERY	7.0	7.8
ORG. PROCESSES		
INPUTS		
CAPITAL	4.7	3.8
HUMAN	7.7*	6.9
INFORMATION	7.2	8.5*
PROCESSING		
COMPUTER	5.7	5.1
MECHANICAL	3.5	4.7
HUMAN	8.5*	9.4*
OUTPUTS		
PRODUCTS	6.5	5.9
SERVICES	7.9*	7.3
BENEFITS	7.3	8.0*
FEEDBACKING		
MONITORING	5.9	5.1
RECYCLING	5.4	5.3
SELF-MANAGEMENT	7.6*	8.0*

*Top-rated dimension in category

of the resource component, information inputs and consumer benefits. In general, their ratings were consistent with consumer-oriented governments that were responsible for producing and supporting human resources and were not accountable for profit-making components like production, marketing and distributing.

Sources of Productivity: Summary and Conclusions

The major findings of this survey may be summarized. Currently, and perhaps increasingly during the Information Age, the following sources of productivity dominate the growing organization:

1. Marketing is the dominant organizational component.
2. Management is the critical organizational function.
3. Human processing is the dominant organizational process.

Let us examine these findings in greater detail.

Organizational Components

The emphasis upon the marketing component represents a shift from the production component which dominated the Industrial Age and the resource component which emerged as critical during the Electronics Era (1960–1980). Put together with the open-ended responses of the C.E.O.'s, the reassertion of the marketing component seems to be saying: "The essence of the Age of Information is to stay finely tuned to consumer requirements through extraordinary marketing efforts." Marketing has a unique meaning in the Age of Information moving from keeping fingers on the pulses of the consumers on the front end through product development in the middle to distributing products and services and providing consumer benefits on the back end of business. To be sure, the marketer is at the critical point of information flow for both consumer input and feed-back on products and services. Actually, the salesperson who enters the consumers' frames of reference provides the critical information to product development and marketing design.

Organizational Functions

The preeminence of the management function presents an interesting paradox. While policy making dominated the Industrial Age, management shot into prominence during the Electronics Era. There is evidence from other quarters to indicate that both responsibility and authority to process in-formation and make decisions is being pushed downward to delivery personnel through decentralization. Yet here are the opinions of the C.E.O.'s of the fastest-growing corpora-tions saying that management is the critical function. Per-haps the resolution of this apparent conflict lies in three prospective movements: (1) the elevation of the skills and responsibilities of managers; (2) the concurrent elevation of the skills and prestige of personnel in the delivery role with the introduction of self-management techniques; (3) the gradual elimination of mid-management and supervision.

Organizational Processes

The findings concerning organizational processes revolve around human processing. The human resource inputs sup-port human processing. The human processing is dedicated to customer service outputs. The feedbacking is intended to elevate the human resources through self-management.

Resource Inputs

The capital and natural resource inputs that dominated the Industrial Age were displaced by human resource in-puts during the Electronics Era. Now, in the Information

Age, human resource development as art is brought to HRD as science with personnel being skilled in productively processing information.

Productive Processing

Whereas non-intelligent mechanical processing dominated the Industrial Age and computer processing emerged in the Electronics Era, now human processing comes into ascendancy in the Age of Information. Personnel skilled in processing or productive thinking skills will transform data into responses that produce products, services and benefits. Human processing emphasizes the synergistic interaction of human and information resources (Carkhuff, 1983, 1984; Carkhuff and Cannon, 1986).

Results Outputs

The products that once dominated the Industrial Age were eclipsed by a customer service orientation during the Electronics Era. Now, increasingly, during the Information Age, the services are seen linked to consumer benefits.

Information Feedback

The Industrial Age use of feedback was to monitor performance. The Electronics Era use of feedback was to improve performance. The Information Age use of feedback is to equip the personnel with the information which they need to manage their own performance.

Conclusions

In conclusion, in this Age of Information, the sources of productivity of the fastest-growing corporations are changing with the successive waves of information. In this context, the C.E.O.'s of the fastest growing organizations offer the following propositions:

1. Marketing is the central component in the information flow in the Information Age.
2. Upper levels of management emphasizing strategic and operations planning are increasingly critical while lower levels of management emphasizing supervision are increasingly anachronistic and/or vestigial.
3. Human processing is the prepotent organizational process for which all other processes are supportive.

Marketing means that fast-growing corporations will capitalize upon constantly changing consumer information. Management means that planners will rapidly transform this information into new product lines, customer services and consumer benefits. Human processing means that all personnel—executive as well as delivery personnel—must learn to think productively so that they can transform information inputs into highly productive response outputs.

V.
Summary and
Transition

11.
Human Processing and Human Productivity

About a century ago, in the middle of the Industrial Revolution, there were "...increasing anxieties in...learned societies and journals that the engineers would use up with their applications what the scholars saw as a reservoir of general ideas" (Morison and Bowser, 1985). "What should they do to refresh those reservoirs of ideas?" they asked.

Today, at the beginning of the Age of Information, we must be concerned with the ability of our social systems to supply the engineers and technicians in such a way as to implement the constant and burgeoning flow of ideas: "What should we do to support the reservoirs of ideas?" we ask.

To both questions, we may answer: "Learn to think productively."

Sources of Economic Growth

Historically, capital and natural resources accounted for the great majority of growth in productivity. Today, they account for a small minority of productivity growth. For example, in the first part of the century, capital and natural resources, including minerals, energy and land, accounted for approximately 75% of our gross national product (GNP). Today, they account for less than one-fourth of GNP.

Human and information resources are the great sources of productivity in the Information Age. Since the early 1900s, these resources have become increasingly dominant in relation to capital and natural resources. Improved quality and reconfiguration of labor through education, training, retraining and "on-the-job know-how" have consistently accounted for the greatest amount of productivity improvement and growth in national income. In general, the higher the quality of human and information resources, the higher the growth in productivity.

When economists project the sources of economic growth, they conceive of factor or resource inputs and productivity components or organizational processing as the dominant sources (Carnavale, 1983; Denison, 1979; Grayson, 1980; Kendrick, 1979). The resource input sources emphasize human and capital resources. The organizational processing sources include information resources or advancements in knowledge and human resources or, in their terms, skilled labor. In turn, the human resources are accounted for primarily by education and training and secondarily by health and workforce composition.

The moderate to high projections in national income range from 3.4% to 4.8% over the 1980–1990 period. The resource inputs account for between 1.8% and 2.2% of this growth. In turn, the organizational processing accounts for from 1.6% to 2.6% of the growth. In general, we may think of the input and processing component contributions as being approximately equal. However, the inputs decrease in contribution and the processing increases in contribution as the productivity growth projections increase. In other words, the higher the productivity growth, the greater is the influence of the organizational processing component.

Thus, we may summarize the sources of projected economic growth as in Figure 11-1. As can be seen, economic growth is accounted for by the resource inputs and organizational processing: the inputs and the processing each account for approximately 50% of the variability in projected economic growth.

$$\text{Economic Growth} = 50\% \text{ Resource Inputs} + 50\% \text{ Organizational Processing}$$

Figure 11-1. Equation for Economic Growth

When we analyze the resource input components, we find that human resources account for the greatest percent of effect. In general, human resources account for around two-thirds or 67% of the input components while capital resources account for around one-third or 33% of the input components. Other factors such as natural resources and land make negligible contributions.

It is important to understand that the human resource inputs to the organization system are outputs of other systems, particularly education and training, but also the home and community. Thus, the human resource inputs bring with them skills, knowledge and attitudes based upon previous learning experiences. In other words, the current mode of analyzing resource inputs incorporates information resources within the human resources.

Thus, we may represent the equation for resource inputs as in Figure 11-2. For purposes of calculation, if we allocate the amount of variance ascribed to human resources equally

$$\text{Resource Inputs} = 33\% \text{ Human Resources} + 33\% \text{ Information Resources} + 33\% \text{ Capital Resources}$$

Figure 11-2. Equation for Resource Inputs

to both human and information resources, we have an approximation of the relative impact of these factors: the human, information and capital resources contribute about equally as resource inputs. It is important to keep in mind that the resource inputs, in total, contribute approximately 50% of the variance to overall economic growth. For our purposes, we may say that human, information and capital resource inputs each contribute in the range of 15%–20% of overall economic growth.

In turn, the organizational processing component breaks down to human and information resource factors. Advancements in knowledge or "working smarter" account for around half of productivity growth. The quality of labor or personnel accounts for the other half with the effects of some "depressor variables" subtracting from the net effects of knowledge and personnel quality. In addition, there is some tendency for the effects of information resources or knowledge to increase as the size of the growth projections increase. In other words, the more efficiently and effectively the personnel work, the greater the growth in productivity.

In short, there is a relationship between human and information resources. As the skills of the human resources improve, the power of the information resources increases. Conversely, as the advancements in knowledge take place, the personnel are empowered. Together, human and information resources maintain a synergistic relationship where

Organizational Processing (HRD ⟷ IRD)	=	50% Human Resource Development	+	50% Information Resource Development

Figure 11–3. Equation for Organizational Processing

each contributes to the growth of the other and both contribute to the productivity growth of the organization.

Thus, we may represent the equation for organizational processing as in Figure 11-3. As can be seen, human and information resources, alone and in interaction (⟷) with each other, contribute equally to organizational processing. Again, for purposes of calculation, we may say that human and information resource processing components each contribute about 25% to overall economic growth.

In summary, we may postulate human and information resources as the prepotent sources of effect in economic growth. High quality human and information resource inputs account for approximately 30%–35% of overall economic growth. Human and information resource processing account for approximately 50% of overall economic growth. Together, human and information resources, alone as inputs and processes, and together in synergistic interaction with each other, account for 80% to 85% of projected economic growth in the Age of Information.

We may represent an equation for the various sources of economic growth as in Figure 11-4. As can be seen, the

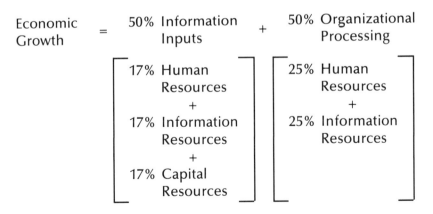

Figure 11–4. Equation for Sources of Economic Growth

human, information and capital resources contribute equally to the 50% of economic growth attributed to resource inputs. In addition, human and information resources, alone and in interaction with each other, account for the 50% of economic growth attributed to organizational processing. In addition, human and information resources, alone and in interaction with each other, account for the 50% of economic growth attributed to organizational processing. Again, we should remember that the greater the economic growth the more potent a contributor is organizational processing (HRD ⟷ IRD). Indeed, we may conjecture that the more robust the organizational processing the greater the economic growth.

Sources of Human and Information Resource Development

It is important to understand not only the ingredients of economic growth but also the sources of these ingredients. We must attempt to answer the critical questions: What are the sources of the human and information resource variables which account for 80%–85% of projected economic growth? How can we impact human and information resource development to facilitate their contributions to economic growth? In other words, we may posit that individual and interpersonal processing account about equally for human and information resource development. It simply

$$\begin{array}{ccc} \text{Organizational} \\ \text{Processing} & = & \text{50\% Individual} & + & \text{50\% Interpersonal} \\ \text{(HRD} \longleftrightarrow \text{IRD)} & & \text{Processing} & & \text{Processing} \end{array}$$

Figure 11–5. Equation for Human Processing

makes good sense that people process, first, independently and then, simultaneously while processing interpersonally or interdependently with others.

From our own research, we have found interpersonal and individual skills each accounting for approximately 50% of the variability in the human and information processing (HRD ←→ IRD) which defines organizational processing. We may represent our equation for human resource development as in Figure 11-5. As can be seen, individual and interpersonal processing contribute about equally to the synergistic interaction of human and information resources which defines human and information resource development in organizational processing.

In addition, we may explore the relationship of education and training to human and information resource development. First, we may attribute the variability of human resource inputs to previous educational experiences in the home and in school. Second, we may explore data from the projections of the economists for the human and information resource development which occurs within the organizational processing component.

We may represent the equation for human resource development within the organizational processing components as in Figure 11-6. As can be seen, education and training account for approximately 80% of human resource development, while health and workforce composition each account for approximately 10%. For our purposes, of the

$$\text{Human Resource Development} = \text{80\% Education \& Training} + \text{10\% Health} + \text{10\% Workforce Composition}$$

Figure 11–6. Equation for Human Resource Development

overall economic growth, education and training accounts for the great majority of the effects of human resource development within the organizational processing component.

Thus, between human and information resource inputs and processing, we may conclude that education and training account for more than 50% of human and information resource development: 35%, human and information resource inputs; and nearly all of the 25% of human resource development within the organizational processing component.

Finally, we may draw upon our research in other areas of human relations to understand the sources of training effectiveness (Carkhuff, 1969, 1983, 1984). We have found that the most critical variables emphasize the trainer's level of functioning in the skills area being taught. Thus, the productive trainer is not only able to teach didactically but, most important, to model representatively the skills being taught. The remaining variance may be attributed to the development and organization of the content and the management of the learners' experiential exercising of the skills.

We may treat education and training in much the same manner as organizational productivity growth. In the instance of training, the training outputs focus upon the gain in trainee acquisition, application and transfer of responses (Carkhuff, 1969, 1983, 1984). Thus, training emphasizes transforming naive human resources into developed or skilled human resources.

We may represent an equation for the effects of training as in Figure 11-7. As can be seen, the critical sources of training are the training resource inputs and the training process itself. Our own research on the effects of training supports the trainers and trainees along with the content they are processing as the critical sources of effect—in the 80% to 85% range—in training gains. In this context, there is evidence to suggest that the prepotent source of effect is the discrepancy between the trainer's and the trainee's initial levels of functioning in the substantive area. In general,

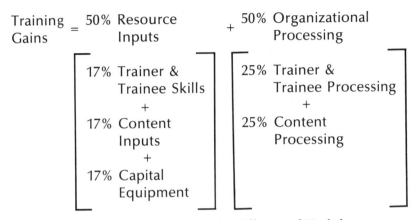

Figure 11-7. Equation for Effects of Training

the trainees gain about one-half of the discrepancy between their levels of functioning and those of the trainers.

Toward Human Processing and Human Productivity

What do these equations for human and information resource development as the sources of economic growth sum to? We may view the critical variables from a different perspective (see Figure 11-8). As can be seen, education and training accounts for most of individual and interpersonal processing which, in turn, accounts for the vast majority of the human and information resource development variables. In turn, human and information resource variables, alone and in synergistic interaction, account for nearly all of

149

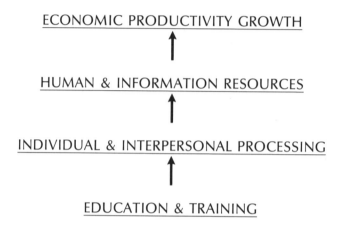

Figure 11–8. Sources of Human Processing

economic productivity. In short, there is nearly a direct-line progression from education to economic growth.

We may place the sources of human productivity in a still larger perspective (see Figure 11-9). The interaction of education and the home may be seen as the source of individual and interpersonal processing skills ($IPS_1 \longleftrightarrow IPS_2$) which account for human and information resource development ($HRD \longleftrightarrow IRD$). In turn, human and information resource development are the primary sources of economic productivity growth and, it is conjectured, human freedom. Together, economic productivity and freedom are the primary sources of peace and prosperity in our "global village."

As citizens of an increasingly smaller world, we may conjecture about the relationships of economic productivity and social and political freedom. The relationships may be

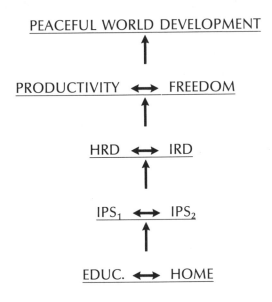

Figure 11–9. Sources of Human Productivity

reasoned logically by observing the differential in productivity in the free and totalitarian systems in the world. A few people simply cannot do the processing required of the many. In short, a free people are a productive people and vice versa.

This is not an ideological but rather a data-based debate. The economic theories of capitalism, communism and, indeed, most modern economic theories are, at best, irrelevant to today's human- and information-based economies. In this context, it is important to respect—not revere—the past. Ninety-nine percent of the ideation in the history of humankind is occurring right now! It is absurd to follow theorists who—however brilliant—had less than one percent of the data which is currently available.

151

Instead of traditional economic conditions, we can envision a succession of volcanic-like eruptions of scientific breakthroughs and innovative technologies, thus creating entirely new sources of economic growth. The entrepreneurial and intrepreneurial explosions which follow cannot be accounted for by traditional theories which account for less and less of the variance in economic growth.

The relationship between economic growth and employment growth is also a changing relationship. The expanding employment opportunities generated by the entrepreneurial organizations contrasts vividly with the declining opportunities provided by large, established corporations. Transitionally, such relationships, typified by "Okun's law," are critical to healthy societies: unemployment declines as the economy expands beyond projected growth rates. However, with the extraordinary leverage of human processing, we must anticipate a time when economic productivity is so enormous that unemployment will not be of concern. Indeed, ultimately, we may envision the day when leisure will be the human mode and work may be a unique outlet for those seeking human fulfillment.

The precondition for this growth is human processing. The critical variables emphasize productive processing skills in interaction with the freedom to create. In this context, free enterprise in a free marketplace for organizations and nations is analogous to free choice for individuals.

The hope for prosperity and peace through productive world development lies in increasing both the freedom to create and the productivity to support this freedom: to make the pie large enough to enable the disenfranchised peoples of the world to themselves become free and productive for their own purposes. All of this revolves around an evolving concept of human productivity. Economic productivity involves not only reducing resource investments while increasing results benefits. It emphasizes consumer productivity. Not only do we deliver products and services to consumers. We also deliver benefits. The core benefit is to help the consumers to become more productive at whatever it is they are about. Whether we are parents or teachers, business persons, government officials or community leaders, our business is to help our consumers stay in business. Consumer productivity is the guiding ethic of all human processing and, indeed, human endeavors.

At the other end of a human productivity delivery system, we must view the parenting—home, family and community— which provides the human resources that are inputs to education. Currently, the home and family backgrounds account for most of the variance in the human resources exiting the secondary school systems in our country. In other words, learner pre-instructional variables relate very highly with learner post-instructional variables. However, when school personnel interact intensely with home, family and community components, schools can elevate their ability to account for as much as 50% of the variability in learner resource development.

In summary, when each component of a human productivity delivery system brings itself into intimate and intense relations with the other components, then a systems synergy can produce exponentially more than the sum of the contributions of its components. Each part can impact every other part productively. Each healthy player can contribute more than his or her share through productive human processing. This human processing is the great source of human productivity. Indeed, this is the potentially infinite source of infinite human productivity leading to a productive, free and peaceful world.

Toward Personal Growth

The pursuit of science is at once grand and enobling, yet highly problematic and humbling. It is an attempt to explicate the unknown—to make the unknown knowable. It is pursued through a mixture of data and research, of interpretation and meaning. Above all, its source is human experience, its gaps are filled by human intuition and are bridged by human conjecture.

There are no longer any laws of science—there never were! There are merely probabilities which serve to guide us to better or more productive probability statements. These formulas for probabilities are pursued by people who are in part disinterested scholars and in part committed artists.

Even Einstein summarized blackboards and books full of data in an artistic equation for communicating a profound yet commercial formula for energy potential: $E = mc^2$. In a similar manner, all scientists—in fact, all people in the Age of Information, for all people are processors—must analyze, synthesize and operationally define, and then creatively communicate productive information.

All people—like scientists—must live their lives, learn their substance, work their jobs, fulfill their potential just as they test human experience: as tentative hypotheses to be supported or qualified or rejected according to the results of their testing, not in research, but in their momentary experience.

All people—like scientists—must be prepared to change their hypotheses and, thus, their lives with the results of their testing, for the Age of Information is, indeed, just that: an era of enormous information flow which comes to us from all points of our universes—internal as well as external—and at all times in our experience—sleeping as well as waking—human as well as extra-human.

In previous eras, people coined the expression, "the Man." There was, indeed, "the Man." He led the tribes of hunter-gatherers, directed the families of farmers, managed the assembly lines of industry. We even conceptualized the possibility of creating a new, computer-based "man," born of expert systems and reared in the artificial intelligence systems of the Electronics Era.

In the Information Age, information is "the Man." "The Man" brings its own meaning, carries its own ethics, dictates its own direction. We need only receive this information lovingly and process it systematically, and we will share in the excitement of birth and maturity, death and rebirth. As with the growth of productive information, we may grow forever.

It is certain that information is our life. To the extent we use our brains to process information, to that same extent do we ensure the building of potent, intense and enduring neurons which define human life—for now and evermore. To the degree that we use information to empower people to make free and productive choices in their lives, to that same degree do we facilitate the movement of civilization into a great new Age of Ideation.

APPENDIX

Bibliography

1. Human Conditioning and Human Crises

Carkhuff, R.R. *Sources of Human Productivity*. Amherst, Mass.: Human Resource Development Press, 1983.

Carkhuff, R.R. *The Exemplar—The Exemplary Performer in the Age of Information*. Amherst, Mass.: Human Resource Development Press, 1984.

Carkhuff, R.R. and Berenson, B.G. *A Psychology of Transition*. Amherst, Mass.: Carkhuff Institute of Human Technology, 1986.

2. Individual Processing Through the Ages

Anderson, J.R. *Language, Memory and Thought*. Hillsdale, N.J.: Erlbaum, 1976.

Atkinson, R.C. "Mnemotechnics in Second-Language Learning," *American Psychologist*, 1975, *30*, 821–828.

Atkinson, R.C. and Estes, W.K. "Stimulus Sampling Theory." In R.D. Luce, R.R. Bush and E. Galanter, Editors, *Handbook of Mathematical Psychology, Volume 2*. New York: Wiley, 1963.

Ausubel, D.P. "The Use of Advance Organizers in the Learning and Retention of Meaningful Verbal Learning." *Journal of Educational Psychology*, 1960, *51*, 267–272.

Bourne, L.E. *Human Conceptual Behavior*. Boston: Allyn and Bacon, 1966.

Bower, G.H. "Partial and Correlated Reward in Escape Learning." *Journal of Experimental Psychology*, 1960, *59*, 126–130.

Bower, G.H. and Hilgard, E.R. *Theories of Learning.* Englewood Cliffs, N.J.: Prentice-Hall, 1981.

Bruner, J.S. *Beyond the Information Given.* New York: Norton, 1972.

Bugelski, B.R. *The Psychology of Learning.* New York: Holt, Rinehart and Winston, 1956.

Bugelski, B.R. *Principles of Learning and Memory.* New York: Praeger, 1979.

Calfee, R.C. and Drum, P.A. "Learning to Read: Theory, Research and Practice." *Curriculum Inquiries*, 1978, *8*, 183–249.

Carkhuff, R.R. *Sources of Human Productivity.* Amherst, Mass.: Human Resource Development Press, 1983.

Carkhuff, R.R. *The Exemplar—The Exemplary Performer in the Age of Productivity.* Amherst, Mass.: Human Resource Development Press, 1984.

Carkhuff, R.R. *Productive Thinking Skills.* Amherst, Mass.: Human Resource Development Press, 1986.

Carkhuff, R.R. and Berenson, B.G. *The Psychology of Transition.* Amherst, Mass.: Carkhuff Institute of Human Technology, 1986. (a)

Carkhuff, R.R. and Berenson, D.H. *Learning-to-Learn.* Amherst, Mass.: Carkhuff Institute of Human Technology, 1981.

Carterette, T.S. "An Application of Stimulus Sampling Theory to Summated Generalization." *Journal of Experimental Psychology*, 1961, *62*, 448–455.

Chomsky, N. In M. Piatelli-Palmarin, Editors. *Language and Learning: Debate Between Piaget and Chomsky.* Cambridge, Mass.: Harvard, 1980.

Deutsch, J.A. and Deutsch, E. *Physiological Psychology.* Homewood, Ill.: Dorsey, 1973.

Estes, W.K. *Learning Theory and Mental Development.* New York: Academic Press, 1970.

Furst, B. *Stop Forgetting: How to Develop Your Memory and Put It To Practical Use*. Garden City, N.Y.: Doubleday, 1958.

Gagne, R.M. *The Conditions of Learning*. New York: Holt, Rinehart and Winston, 1965.

Gagne, R.M. and Briggs, L.J. *Principles of Instructional Design*. New York: Holt, Rinehart and Winston, 1974.

Gallagher, J. and Reid, D. *The Learning Theory of Piaget and Innhelder*. Monterey, Calif.: Brooks/Cole, 1981.

Gates, A.I. "Recitation as a Factor in Memorizing." *Archives of Psychology, N.Y.*, 1917, *40*, 6.

Goodwin, D.L. and Coates, T.J. *Helping Students Help Themselves*. Englewood Cliffs, N.J.: Prentice-Hall, 1976.

Guthrie, E.R. *The Psychology of Learning*. New York: Harper and Row, 1952.

Hebb, D.O. *The Organization of Behavior*. New York: Wiley, 1949.

Hilgard, E. and Bower, G. *Theories of Learning*. Englewood Cliffs, N.J.: Prentice-Hall, 1975. (4th ed.)

Hilgard, E. and Marquis, B.G. *Conditioning and Learning*. New York: Appleton-Century-Crofts, 1961.

Hull. C.L. *Essentials of Behavior*. New Haven: Yale University Press, 1951.

Katona, G. *Organizing and Memorizing*. New York: Columbia University Press, 1940.

Kimble, D.P. *Physiological Psychology*. Reading, Mass.: Addison-Wesley, 1963.

Kimble, G.A. *Hilgard and Marquis' Conditioning and Learning*. New York: Appleton-Century-Crofts, 1961.

Kintsch, W. and VanDijk, T.A. "Toward a Model of Text Comprehension and Production." *Psychological Review*, 1979, *85*, 363–394.

Kohler, W. *The Mentality of Apes*. New York: Harcourt, Brace and World, 1925.

Koffka, K. *Principles of Gestalt Psychology*. New York: Harcourt, Brace and World, 1935.

LaBerge, D.L. "Generalization Gradients in Discrimination Situation." *Journal of Experimental Psychology*, 1961, *62*, 88–94.

Lepper, M.R. and Green, D., Editors. *The Hidden Costs of Reward.* Hillsdale, N.J.: Erlbaum, 1978.

Lorayne, H. and Lucas, J. *The Memory Book.* New York: Ballantine Books, 1974.

Lovejoy, E. *Attention in Discrimination Learning.* San Fransisco: Holden-Day, 1968.

Mager, R.F. *Preparing Instructional Objectives.* Palo Alto, Calif.: Fearon Publishing, 1972.

Mayer, G.R. and Butterworth, T.N. "A Preventative Approach to School Violence and Vandalism: An Experimental Study." *Personnel and Guidance Journal*, 1979, *57*, 436–441.

Meichenbaum, D. *Cognitive Behavior Modification: An Integrative Approach.* New York: Pelnum Press, 1977.

Meichenbaum, D. and Asarnow, J. "Cognitive Behavior Modification and Metacognitive Development." In P. Kendell and S. Hollon, Editors, *Cognitive Behavior Interventions.* New York: Academic Press, 1979.

Meyer, B. *The Organization of Prose and Its Effect Upon Memory.* Amsterdam: North-Holland, 1975.

Mowrer, O.H. *Learning Theory and the Symbolic Processes.* New York: J. Wiley, 1960.

Norman, D.A. and Rumelhart, D.E., Editors. *Explorations in Cognition.* San Fransisico: W.H. Freeman, 1975.

O'Leary, K.D. and O'Leary, S.G., Editors, *Classroom Management: The Successful Use of Behavior Modification.* New York: Pergamon, 1972.

Osterhouse, R.A. "Group Systematic Desensitization of Test Anxiety." In J.D. Krumboltz and C.E. Thoreson, Editors. *Counseling Methods.* New York: Holt, Rinehart and Winston, 1976.

Packard, R.G. "The Control of Classroom Attention: A Group Contingency for Complex Behavior." *Journal of Applied Behavioral Analysis*, 1970, *3*, 13–28.

Piaget, J. In M. Piatelli-Palmarini, Editors, *Language and Learning: Debate Between Piaget and Chomsky.* Cambridge, Mass.: Harvard, 1980.

Piatelli-Palmarini, M. *Language and Learning.* Cambridge, Mass.: Harvard, 1980.

Restle, F.A. "A Theory of Discrimination Learning." *Psychological Review*, 1955, *62*, 11–19.

Rosenszweig, M.R. and Bennet, E.L., Editors. *Neural Mechanisms of Learning and Motivation*. Cambridge: MIT Press, 1976.

Schank, R.C., Editor, *Conceptual Information Processing*. Amsterdam: North-Holland, 1975.

Schwartz, B. *Psychology of Learning and Behavior*. New York: Norton, 1984.

Skinner, B.F. *Contingencies of Reinforcement*. Englewood Cliffs, N.J.: Prentice-Hall, 1969.

Spence, K.W. *Behavior Theory and Conditioning*. New Haven: Yale University Press, 1956.

Sutherland, N.S. and Macintosh, N.J. *Mechanisms of Animal Discrimination Learning*. New York: Academic Press, 1971.

Thompson, R.F. *Foundations of Physiological Psychology*. New York: Harper & Row, 1967.

Thorndike, E.L. *Human Learning*. New York: Century Paperback, 1931.

Wark, D.M. "Teaching Study Skills to Adults." In J.D. Krumboltz and C.E. Thoreson, Editors, *Counseling Methods*. New York: Holt, Rinehart and Winston, 1976.

Watson, D.L. and Tharp, R.G. *Self-Directed Behavior: Self-Modification for Personal Adjustment*. Monterey, Calif.: Brooks-Cole, 1977.

Wertheimer, M. *Productive Thinking*. New York: Harper and Row, 1959.

Winograd, T. "Understanding Natural Language." *Cognitive Psychology*, 1972, *3*, 1–191.

Wolpe, J. *Psychotherapy by Reciprocal Inhibition*. Stanford: Stanford University Press, 1958.

Zeaman, D. and House, B.J. "The Role of Attention in Retardate Discrimination Learning." In N.R. Ellis, Editor, *Handbook of Mental Deficiency*. New York: McGraw-Hill, 1963.

3. Interpersonal Processing Through the Ages

Carkhuff, R.R. *Helping and Human Relations. Volumes I & II*. New York: Holt, Rinehart and Winston, 1969.

Carkhuff, R.R. *Interpersonal Skills and Human Productivity*. Amherst, Mass.: Human Resource Development Press, 1983.

Carkhuff, R.R. *The Exemplar—The Exemplary Performer in the Age of Productivity*. Amherst, Mass.: Human Resource Development Press, 1984.

Freud, S. *Collected Papers*. London: Hogarth, 1924.

Freud, S. *New Introductory Lectures*. New York: Norton, 1933.

Fromm, E. *Man and Himself*. New York: Holt, Rinehart and Winston, 1947.

Horney, K. *Self-Analysis*. New York: Norton, 1942.

May, R., Editor. *Existential Psychology*. New York: Random House, 1961.

Rogers, C.R. *Client-Centered Therapy*. Boston: Houghton-Mifflin, 1951.

Rogers, C.R. and Dyamond, R.F. *Psychotherapy and Personality Change*. Chicago: University of Chicago Press, 1954.

Sullivan, H.S. "Introduction to the Study of Interpersonal Relations." *Psychiatry*, 1938, Volume 1.

Watson, J.B. *Behavior*. New York: Holt, Rinehart and Winston, 1914.

4. Organizational Processing Through the Ages

Carkhuff, R.R. *The Development of Human Resources*. New York: Holt, Rinehart and Winston, 1971.

Carkhuff, R.R. and Cannon, J.R. *The Exemplary Organization in the Age of Productivity*. Amherst, Mass.: Carkhuff Institute of Human Technology, 1986.

Cyert, R.M. and March J.G. *A Behavioral Theory of the Firm*. Englewood Cliffs, N.J.: Prentice-Hall, 1963.

Drucker, P. *The End of Economic Man*. New York: John Day, 1939.

Drucker, P. *The Future of Industrial Man*. New York: John Day, 1942.

Drucker, P. *The Practice of Management.* New York: Harper and Row, 1954.

Drucker, P. *Management.* New York: Harper and Row, 1974.

Katz, D. and Kahn, R.L. *The Social Psychology of Organizations.* New York: Wiley, 1966.

Likert, R. *New Patterns of Management.* New York: McGraw-Hill, 1961.

March, J.G. and Simon H.A. *Organizations.* New York: Wiley, 1958.

Thompson, J.D. *Organizations in Action: Social Science Bases of Administrative Theory.* New York: McGraw-Hill, 1967.

5. Individual Processing in the Age of Information

Carkhuff, R.R. *Sources of Human Productivity.* Amherst, Mass.: Human Resource Development Press, 1983.

Carkhuff, R.R. *The Exemplar—The Exemplary Performer in the Age of Productivity.* Amherst, Mass.: Human Resource Development Press, 1984.

Carkhuff, R.R. *Productive Thinking Skills. Series.* Amherst, Mass.: Human Resource Development Press, 1986.

Carkhuff, R.R. and Berenson, D.H. *Learning to Learn.* Amherst, Mass.: Carkhuff Institute of Human Technology, 1981.

6. Interpersonal Processing in the Age of Information

Carkhuff, R.R. *Helping and Human Relations. Volumes I & II.* New York: Holt, Rinehart and Winston, 1969.

Carkhuff, R.R. *Interpersonal Skills and Human Productivity.* Amherst, Mass.: Human Resource Development Press, 1983. (a)

Carkhuff, R.R. *Sources of Human Productivity.* Amherst, Mass.: Human Resource Development Press, 1983.

Carkhuff, R.R. *The Exemplar—The Exemplary Performer in the Age of Productivity.* Amherst, Mass.: Human Resource Development Press, 1984.

7. Organizational Processing in the Age of Information

Carkhuff, R.R. *The Exemplar—The Exemplary Performer in the Age of Productivity.* Amherst, Mass.: Human Resource Development Press, 1984.

Carkhuff, R.R. and Cannon, J.R. *The Exemplary Organization in the Age of Information.* Amherst, Mass.: Carkhuff Institute of Human Technology, 1986.

Carnavale, A. *Human Capital.* Washington, D.C.: American Society for Training and Development, 1983.

8. Individual Processing and Individual Performance

Banks, G., Cannon, J.R., Carkhuff, R.R., Friel, T.W., McCune, S. and Pierce, R.M. "Management Systems Designs in Government," Chapter 13. In R.R. Carkhuff, *Sources of Human Productivity.* Amherst, Mass.: Human Resource Development Press, 1983.

Berenson, D.H., Berenson, S.R., Berenson, B.G., Carkhuff, R.R., Griffin, A.H. and Ransom, B.M. "The Physical, Emotional and Intellectual Effects of Teaching Learning Skills To Minority Group Drop-Out Learners." *Research Reports, Carkhuff Institute of Human Technology,* 1978, 2, No. 1.

Carkhuff, R.R. *Interpersonal Skills and Human Productivity.* Amherst, Mass.: Human Resource Development Press, 1983. (a)

Carkhuff, R.R. *Sources of Human Productivity.* Amherst, Mass.: Human Resource Development Press, 1983. (b)

Carkhuff, R.R., Devine, J., Berenson, B.G., Griffin, A.H. *Cry Twice! From Custody to Treatment.* Amherst, Mass.: Human Resource Development Press, 1974.

Collingwood, T., Douds, A., Williams, H. and Wilson, R.D. *Developing Youth Resources.* Amherst, Mass.: Carkhuff Institute of Human Technololgy, 1978.

Danley, K., Ahearn, J. and Battenschlag, J. *Learning Center Report.* Pontiac, Mich.: Pontiac School District, 1975.

Devine, J., Bellingham, R., Essex, G. and Steinberg, H. *Child Care Unit—Year End Report*. Kalamazoo, Mich.: Kalamazoo County Juvenile Home, 1977.

Hall, R. *Comprehensive Skill Training—An Effective Alternative to Traditional Juvenile Correctional Institution Programs*. Mandan, N.D.: North Dakota State Industrial School, 1978. (a)

Hall, R. *A Study of the Physical, Emotional and Intellectual Effects Upon Delinquents of Comprehensive HRD Training*. Mandan, N.D.: North Dakota State Industrial School, 1978. (b)

Kelly, J. *The Effects of IPS Training Upon Word Processing Output*. White Plains, N.Y.: I.B.M., 1983.

Pierce, R.M. "Training in Basic Supervisor Skills: A Report on the Department of Education," Chapter 17. In R.R. Carkhuff, *Sources of Human Productivity*. Amherst, Mass.: Human Resource Development Press, 1983.

Steinberg, H., Bellingham, R. and Devine, J. *The Effects of Systematic HRD Training Upon Ex-offender Adjustment*. Kalamazoo, Mich.: Kalamazoo County Jail, 1981.

Wawrykow, G. "The Effects of Four Models of Learning Upon Learner Acquisition of Skills." *Research Reports, Carkhuff Institute of Human Technology*, 1978, 2, No 2.

9. Interpersonal Processing and Unit Productivity

Brillinger, R. and Friel, T.W. "Productive Management Systems, Chapter 8." In R.R. Carkhuff, *Sources of Human Productivity*. Amherst, Mass.: Human Resource Development Press, 1983.

Carkhuff, R.R. *Sources of Human Productivity*. Amherst, Mass.: Human Resource Development Press, 1983.

Carkhuff, R.R. *Interpersonal Skills and Human Productivity*. Amherst, Mass.: Human Resource Development Press, 1983.

Carkhuff, R.R. *The Exemplar—The Exemplary Performer in the Age of Productivity*. Amherst, Mass.: Human Resource Development Press, 1984.

Carkhuff, R.R. and Cannon, J.R. *The Exemplary Organization in the Age of Productivity.* Amherst,Mass.: Carkhuff Institute of Human Technology, 1986.

Douds, A. *The Effects of IPS-Trained Managers Upon Worker Performance.* San Diego, Calif.: Convair Corp., 1982.

Feder, R. *The Cumulative Effects of IPS-Based Management Applications.* New Orleans, La.: AMOCO, Inc., 1984.

Feder, E. *Productivity Improvement Project.* Houston, Tex.: Tenneco, 1985.

Feeney, E. *Behavioral Engineering Systems Training.* Redding, Conn.: Edward J. Feeney Associates, 1976.

Fournies, F. *Coaching for Improved Work Performance.* New York: Van Nostrand-Reinhold, 1978.

Friel, T.W. and Pierce, R.M. "Systematizing Productive Interventions. Chapter 14." In R.R. Carkhuff, *Sources of Human Productivity.* Amherst, Mass.: Human Resource Development Press, 1983. (a)

Gilbert, T. *Human Competence.* New York: McGraw-Hill, 1978.

Holder, B.T. *The Effects of IPS-Based Performance Management Training.* Anchorage, Alaska: ARCO Alaska, 1982.

McClain, T.W. *Boston Milk Plant Supervisory Development Training. February–May 1982. Summary Report.* Boston: Hood Dairy, 1982.

McClain, T.W. *Wester Dairy Region Supervisory Development Program. September–December 1982. Summary Report.* Boston: Hood Dairy, 1982.

Shultz, J. and Rowe, J. *An Assessment of Interpersonal Skills-Based Management Training.* San Diego, Calif.: Electronics, 1982.

Shultz, J. and Rowe, J. *The Effects of IPS-Based Performance Management Training.* Pomona, Calif.: General Dynamics, 1983.

Zigon, J. "Performance Chain Reactions." *Performance Management Magazine,* 1983, 2, 22–25.

Zigon, J. "Increasing the Bottom Line Results of Training." *Performance and Instruction Journal,* 1984, 18–20.

10. Organizational Processing and Organizational Productivity

Carkhuff, R.R. *Sources of Human Productivity.* Amherst, Mass.: Human Resource Development Press, 1983.

Carkhuff, R.R. *The Exemplar—The Exemplary Performer in the Age of Productivity.* Amherst, Mass.: Human Resource Development Press, 1984.

Carkhuff, R.R. and Cannon, J.R. *The Exemplary Organization in the Age of Productivity.* Amherst, Mass.: Carkhuff Institute of Human Technology, 1986.

Hartman, C. "Who's Running America's Fastest Growing Companies?" *INC.*, August 1983.

Hartman, C. "Inside the INC. 500." *INC.*, December 1984.

Ketchum, B.W. "The INC. 100." *INC.*, May 1984.

Sammons, Donna. "The INC. 100." *INC.*, May 1983.

11. Human Processing and Human Productivity

Carkhuff, R.R. *Helping and Human Relations. Volumes I and II.* New York: Holt, Rinehart & Winston, 1969.

Carkhuff, R.R. *Sources of Human Productivity.* Amherst, Mass.: Human Resource Development Press, 1983.

Carkhuff, R.R. *The Exemplar—The Exemplary Performer in the Age of Productivity.* Amherst, Mass.: Human Resource Development Press, 1984.

Carkhuff, R.R. and Berenson, B.G. *The Psychology of Transition.* Amherst, Mass.: Carkhuff Institute of Human Technology, 1986.

Carkhuff, R.R. and Cannon, J.R. *The Exemplary Organization in the Age of Productivity.* Amherst, Mass.: Carkhuff Institute of Human Technology, 1986.

Carnavale, A.P. *Human Capital.* Washington, D.C.: American Society for Training and Development, 1983.

Morison, E. E. and Bowser, H. "Technology and the Human Dimension." *Invention and Technology*, 1985, *1*, 35–41.